THE LETTER TO THE HEBREWS
IN SOCIAL-SCIENTIFIC PERSPECTIVE

Cascade Companions

The Christian theological tradition provides an embarrassment of riches: from Scripture to modern scholarship, we are blessed with a vast and complex theological inheritance. And yet this feast of traditional riches is too frequently inaccessible to the general reader.

The Cascade Companions series addresses the challenge by publishing books that combine academic rigor with broad appeal and readability. They aim to introduce nonspecialist readers to that vital storehouse of authors, documents, themes, histories, arguments, and movements that comprise this heritage with brief yet compelling volumes.

SELECT TITLES IN THIS SERIES:

Theological Interpretation of Scripture by Stephen E. Fowl

Conflict, Community, and Honor by John H. Elliott

Reading Paul by Michael J. Gorman

Theology and Culture by D. Stephen Long

Creationism and the Conflict over Evolution by Tatha Wiley

Justpeace Ethics by Jarem T. Sawatsky

Reading Bonhoeffer by Geffrey B. Kelly

Christianity and Politics in America by C. C. Pecknold

FORTHCOMING TITLES:

Basil of Caesarea by Andrew Radde-Gallwitz

iPod, YouTube, Wii Play by D. Brent Laytham

Philippians in Context by Joseph H. Hellerman

The Letter to the Hebrews in Social-Scientific Perspective

David A. deSilva

CASCADE *Books* · Eugene, Oregon

THE LETTER TO THE HEBREWS IN SOCIAL-SCIENTIFIC
PERSPECTIVE

Cascade Companions 15

Cascade Books
An Imprint of Wipf and Stock Publishers
199 W. 8th Ave., Suite 3
Eugene, OR 97401

www.wipfandstock.com

ISBN 13: 978-1-60608-855-5

Cataloging-in-Publication data:

deSilva, David Arhtur

    The letter to the Hebrews in social-scientific perspective / David A.
deSilva

    xvi + 188 p. ; 20 cm. Includes bibliographical references and index.

    Cascade Companions 15

    ISBN 13: 978-1-60608-855-5

    1. Bible. N.T. Hebrews—Social scientific criticism. I. Title. II. Series.

BS2775.52 D4 2012

Manufactured in the U.S.A.

In honor of Luke Timothy Johnson,

a generous Doktorvater and exemplary scholar

Contents

Abbreviations

Ancient Works

Aristotle, *Eth. nic.*	*Ethica nichomachea*
Aristotle, *Rhet.*	*Rhetorica*
John Chrysostom,	
Hom. Heb.	*Homiliae in epistulam ad Hebraeos*
Dio Chrysostom, *Or.*	*Orationes*
Dio Chrysostom,	
Philoct.	*Philoctetes*
Epictetus, *Diss.*	*Dissertationes*
Euripedes, *Orest.*	*Orestes*
Eusebius, *Hist. eccl.*	*Historia ecclesiastica*
Fronto, *Ad M. Caes.*	*Ad M. Caesarem*
Gregory of Nyssa,	
Eunom.	*Contra Eunomium*
Herodotus, *Hist.*	*Historiae*
Justin Martyr, *Dial.*	*Dialogus cum Tryphone*
L.A.B.	*Liber antiquitatum biblicarum* (Pseudo-Philo)
Diogenes Laertius,	
Vit. Phil.	*Vitae philosophorum*
Lucian, *Peregr.*	*De morte Peregrini*
Lucian, *Pat. enc.*	*Patriae encomium*

Origen, *Mart.*	*Exhortatio ad Marytrium*
Origen, *Fr. Ps.*	*Fragmenta in Psalmos*
Philo, *Flacc.*	*In Flaccum*
Philo, *Leg.*	*Legum allegoriae*
Philo, *Mos.*	*De vita Mosis*
Philo, *Prob.*	*Quod omnis probus liber sit*
Philo, *Virt.*	*De virtutibus*
Plato *Cri.*	*Crito*
Plato, *Phaedr.*	*Phaedrus*
Pliny, *Ep.*	*Epistulae*
Plutarch, *Exil.*	*De exilio*
Plutarch, *Mor.*	*Moralia*
Rhet. Her.	*Rhetorica ad Herennium*
Seneca, *Ben.*	*De beneficiis*
Seneca, *Constant.*	*De constantia sapientis*
Seneca, *Ep.*	*Epistulae morales*
Seneca, *Prov.*	*De providentia*
Tacitus, *Ann.*	*Annales*

JOURNALS AND SERIES

ACNT	Abingdon New Testament Commentary
BSac	*Bibliotheca sacra*
BTB	*Biblical Theology Bulletin*
BZ	*Biblische Zeitschrift*
CBQ	*Catholic Biblical Quarterly*
CTJ	*Calvin Theological Journal*
HNTC	Harper's New Testament Commentaries
ICC	International Critical Commentary
JBL	*Journal of Biblical Literature*
JSNT	*Journal for the Study of the New Testament*
JSSR	*Journal for the Scientific Study of Religion*
KEK	Kritisch-exegetischer Kommentar über das Neue Testament

NIBCNT	New International Biblical Commentary on the New Testament
NICNT	New International Commentary on the New Testament
NIGTC	New International Greek Testament Commentary
NIVAC	NIV Application Commentary
NTL	New Testament Library
NTS	*New Testament Studies*
RRelRes	*Review of Religious Research*
SJT	*Scottish Journal of Theology*
SNTSMS	Society for New Testament Studies Monograph Series
SNTSU	*Studien zum Neuen Testament und seiner Umwelt*
SP	Sacra pagina
SNT	Studien zum Neuen Testament
TynBul	*Tyndale Bulletin*

Introduction

Guiding Questions for a Social-Scientific Interpretation

The Letter—or, better, the *Sermon*—to the Hebrews offers some of the loftiest theological reflections in the New Testament. Here we read of the exaltation of the Son above every cosmic being, all carefully established with Scriptural support (1:1–14). We find arcane speculation about the shadowy figure of Melchizedek (7:1–10), on the basis of which the author launches into an extended exploration of Jesus' priestly sacrifice in comparison with the sacrifices offered by the Levitical priests in the tabernacle as described in Exodus and Leviticus (7:11—10:18). In what may be the most familiar passage, we read of the heroes of faith across such a broad time span as to become timeless (ch. 11). The author talks so much about the sacred past and the invisible activity in the heavenly realm that we are tempted to forget that he is addressing flesh-and-blood people living somewhere around the Mediterranean basin wrestling with real-life concerns and seeking to come to terms with some very mundane realities in their changing social circumstances, and that he is probably concerned very much with their responses to and within those circumstances.

Social-scientific interpretation provides tools and approaches that help to correct any such tendency in our reading of a particular New Testament text. Grounded in the methods and heuristic models of the social sciences, it helps interpreters enter into the "real-life" social context of the author that created, and the audience intended to receive and respond to, a text.[1] It helps us not lose sight of how a text is informed by the social situation in which it was produced and by which it was, at least in part, evoked, and how the text potentially impacts people living within their social situation. It allows us to connect the ideas and beliefs communicated by a text with the "lived world" of the people producing and receiving the text, and perhaps also the changes within that "lived world" that the text nurtures. When social-scientific interpretation supplements the other varied skills and tools brought to the interpretation of a text, it helps the interpreter discover the flesh behind the word. This is especially important where biblical interpretation happens in contexts where people continue to seek guidance for their own flesh-and-blood lives and communities in this same word.

An important aim of social-scientific criticism, including the cultural-anthropological study of the first-century Greco-Roman world, is to lay bare the cultural and social distance between the modern readers and interpreters, on the one hand, and the ancient authors and audiences, on the other.[2] We seek to discover the "given" roles and logic of their

1. Some helpful surveys of research in this area and bibliographic guides include Holmberg, *Sociology and the New Testament*; Elliott, *Social-Scientific Criticism*, 138–74; Harrington, "Second Testament Exegesis and the Social Sciences"; Horrell, *Social-Scientific Approaches*.

2. Elliott, *Social-Scientific Criticism*, 38; deSilva, *Honor, Patronage, Kinship & Purity*, 17–21.

social customs and institutions and their cultural norms, so that we may read these ancient texts in the context of the presuppositions and shared knowledge that the ancient authors and audiences brought to these texts as acts of communication, rather than impose our own presuppositions and cultural knowledge upon the same. We will see just how important this is, for example, in the fourth chapter when we read Hebrews in light of "grace" and the expectations and ethos of grace relationships in the first-century Greco-Roman environment, which is very different from the modern, post-Reformation environment.

Social-scientific criticism invites the formulation of new questions, and thus the potential discovery of new data in the texts and their environment, or at least new ways of analyzing the data to which we already have access.[3] The explorations undertaken in this companion to Hebrews can be correlated with several of the particular questions that John H. Elliott formulated as avenues into sociological exegesis. In the first chapter, we will explore author-centered questions: "Who is the explicitly mentioned or implied *author-sender* of the text? If the document is anonymous, what can be inferred about the author's identity and on what basis? . . . What is the relationship of intended audience and author-sender(s)?"[4] While the question of the identity of the author of Hebrews is ultimately unsolvable, his sermon provides ample material for the creation of a social profile. We will focus particularly on the level and nature of his education, his degree of acculturation

3. See the lists of questions for guiding sociological investigations of texts compiled in Kee, *Knowing the Truth*, 65–69; Elliott, *Social-Scientific Criticism*, 72–74, 110–23; deSilva, *Introduction to the New Testament*, 438–44, 629–31, 650–52, 831–38.

4. Elliott, *Social-Scientific Criticism*, 74.

to the Hellenistic-Roman environment, and the nature of his authority in the community.

The second chapter focuses on audience-centered questions: "Who are the explicitly mentioned (or implied) *readers-hearers* of this document? What is their geographical location? What is their social composition? . . . Can a social profile of the audience be constructed?"[5] Again, historical investigation alone comes up short in regard to the audience of Hebrews, since their location cannot be determined with any confidence. Nevertheless, sifting through Hebrews with the kinds of questions social-scientific exegesis brings to a text allows us to analyze the clues that *are* given in regard to the community's ethnic composition, the community's formative history, and its members' social level.

The question of primary importance for interpreting any occasional text like a letter or a written sermon concerns what was going on the community's situation to occasion such a response? Hence we also need to ask: "How is the *social situation* described in the text? What information is explicitly provided or implied? What information is stressed through repetition, reformulation, or emphatic placement? Can further information on the situation be supplied from external sources? How does the author *diagnose and evaluate* the situation? What phenomena are singled out for approval, commendation, disapproval, condemnation, or necessary change?"[6] It is all too tempting to look in the realm of theological ideas or, perhaps, ethical deviations for the presenting cause of an epistle, and thus conclude that the author of Hebrews is primarily concerned about a deficient Christology among his hearers, or

5. Ibid., 72.
6. Ibid., 73.

a dangerous fascination with non-Christian Judaism. Social-scientific exegesis reminds us that social factors may be just as, if not more, important and pressing.

Chapters 3 through 5, then, seek to understand how the sermon is strategically constructed to address the particular challenges that the author identifies, and to motivate the audience to respond in the way that the author desires: "What *response* does the author seek from the targeted audience? . . . How does the author attempt to *motivate and persuade* the audience? To what shared goals, values, norms, sanctions, and traditions is appeal made? . . . Are any dominant symbols or 'root metaphors' used to characterize and express the collective identity and action of the audience? How is the document constituted to be an effective instrument of rhetorical persuasion and social interaction?"[7] It is this focus on how a text's rhetoric is directed to effect social responses that accounts for the use of the term "sociorhetorical" in the titles of these chapters. Throughout these explorations, we are also concerned with questions about ideology and interests—the interests of the Christians' neighbors, the varied interests among the audience, and the author's interests—and how the author uses the ideological tools at his disposal to make the best interests of the group (namely, its survival in an unsupportive-to-hostile environment) displace any competing interests.

These studies are offered not only in the hope of contributing to the task of helping the Sermon to the Hebrews take on flesh and blood for contemporary readers, but also to the task of expanding the readers' tools for exploring other texts, asking fresh kinds of questions and discovering fresh dimensions in the situations and responses reflected therein.

7. Ibid., 73–74.

ONE

The Author of Hebrews: A Social Profile

Hebrews is an anonymous sermon, which poses something of a challenge to creating a full-bodied social profile. The mention of Timothy in Heb 13:23, combined with Paul's reputation as a letter writer, led early scribes to begin to attribute the letter to Paul, which aided greatly in its eventual acceptance into the canon. Only after Jerome and Augustine championed the cause of Pauline authorship did this view take deep roots, however. Second- and third-century Christian leaders like Clement of Alexandria, Origen, and Tertullian believed that a member of Paul's team, and not Paul himself, had authored this epistle, or in Origen's famous judgment, "who truly wrote the letter only God knows" (quoted in Eusebius, *Hist. eccl.* 6.25.14).

Several factors strongly argue against attributing the sermon to Paul. First, the author includes himself among those who came to faith through the preaching of other apostles

(Heb 2:3–4). This is perhaps the strongest argument against Pauline authorship, for Paul adamantly insists that he came to faith through a direct intervention by Jesus and *not* through any human being's words (see Gal 1:11–17; 1 Cor 15:3–10). Second, none of the writings bearing Paul's name come close to the rhetorical finesse and stylistic polish of Hebrews. Indeed, Paul explicitly refused to rely on well-crafted rhetoric ("the loftiness of words or wisdom," 1 Cor 2:1),[1] lest persuasion come through the speaker's art rather than the Spirit's conviction (1 Cor 2:1–5). The author of Hebrews clearly had a different philosophy of preaching than did Paul. Third, although the sermon shares many topics with Paul (the examples of Abraham and Jesus, the Mosaic covenant), they are often developed in different ways. The author's focus on Jesus as high priest and on the Israelite cult, moreover, is quite distinctive.[2] Finally, the debates over the letter's canonicity themselves attest to the fact that Paul's name was not attached to the letter from the beginning, either in writing or by tradition. If it were written by Paul, there would not have been such discussions concerning authorship and questions concerning canonicity as we find before the Synod of Hippo (393 CE).[3]

Based on their observation that Hebrews differed from Paul's letters in rhetorical style and content, Clement, Origen, and Tertullian suggested alternative candidates from among the Pauline team: Barnabas and Apollos often emerged as

1. Translations of biblical texts are the author's own unless otherwise noted.

2. At one point, however, Paul provides precisely the sort of seed that a colleague could have developed as does the author of Hebrews: "Christ . . . who is at the right hand of God, who intercedes on our behalf" (Rom 8:34).

3. Salevao, *Legitimation*, 97.

favorites. Nevertheless, the case for any particular member of the Pauline circle will always remain inconclusive and, largely, circumstantial.[4]

LEVEL OF EDUCATION

Though we lack a name to attach to this sermon, the author reveals enough of himself to provide at least a partial social profile.[5] First, he is well educated. Whether he acquired this formally or informally cannot ultimately be demonstrated, but he acquired the level of rhetorical proficiency that formal training sought to nurture and has, perhaps, a better claim to formal education than any other New Testament author. It is particularly striking to find the author using patterns of argumentation that follow—literally—standard "textbook" exercises. Before advanced study of rhetoric and oratory, young students would be introduced to more elementary exercises in logic, composition, and speech writing called the *Progymnasmata*, or *Preliminary Exercises*. Several textbooks

4. See, further, discussions of authorship in Attridge, *Hebrews*, 1–5; deSilva, *Perseverance*, 23–25; Koester, *Hebrews*, 42–46; Lane, *Hebrews 1–9*, lxvii–li.

5. I use the masculine pronoun to refer to the author, following the author's own practice. He uses the masculine form of a participle when referring to himself as the subject of the participial action (11:32). This argues definitively against attempts to attribute the sermon to Priscilla. It is highly unlikely to have been a mistake, given the author's excellent grasp of Greek (and his own gender). The early church was quite open to female leadership, removing any need for a female author to "disguise" her gender. Even if there were issues in this regard, however, the author indicates that he is personally known to the audience and even plans to come visit them shortly (13:23), hence cannot expect to trick them into accepting the authority of the message on the basis of a misleading participle.

from the first through fourth centuries CE survive, giving us direct access to what was taught at this level.[6] Several of the exercises involved mastering a pattern called "elaboration," a pattern applied to a thesis, a proposition, or a famous statement by a famous person (the last is called a *chreia*). The elaboration pattern took a student through many of the basic building blocks of rhetorical argumentation, building blocks that would be used to construct arguments for the rest of his public life.

According to the *Progymnasmata* attributed to Hermogenes (second century CE), the exercise began with the recitation of a maxim or *chreia* and involved developing a full argument in support of the maxim or saying according to the following outline:

1. Introduction
2. Statement of *chreia* (or maxim)
3. Cause (reason, rationale)
4. Contrast (contrary)
5. Comparison (analogy)
6. Example (historical precedent)
7. A judgment (quotation of an authority)
8. Concluding exhortation/restatement[7]

A very similar pattern appears in the anonymous *Rhetorica ad Herennium*, an advanced handbook on rhetoric from the early first century BCE, as a useful way to develop any theme (any thesis or exhortation) that might arise in the course of a speech:

6. These are conveniently collected in Kennedy, *Progymnasmata*.

7. Hermogenes, *Progymnasmata* 3.7–8; see also 4.10. The text can be found in Kennedy, *Progymnasmata*, 77–78.

2. Thesis
3. Cause (reason, rationale)
– Restatement of theme in another form (with or without reasons)
4. Contrast (contrary)
5. Comparison (analogy)
6. Historical Example (precedent)
7. Concluding exhortation/restatement

Each of these elements may include a more fully developed argument with its own rationales, as the sample elaboration that follows in the textbook shows (*Rhet. Her.* 4.43.56—4.44.57).

When the author of Hebrews turns to talk about God's formative discipline—the education God provides the congregation through the trials they have endured—he uses precisely this pattern, with the kind of variation one would expect in actual practice:

> *Introduction* (12:5a):
> You have forgotten the exhortation which
>   addresses you as sons:
>
> *Thesis/Chreia* (12:5b):
> "My son, do not regard lightly the formative
>   discipline [*paideia*] of the Lord,
> nor lose courage while being reproved by him.
>
> *Rationale* (12:6):
> For whom the Lord loves, he disciplines,
> and chastens every son whom he receives."
>
> *Restatement of Thesis* (12:7a):
> Endure for the sake of formative discipline.
>
> *Restatement of Rationale* (12:7b):
> God is treating you as sons.

Confirmation of Rationale (12:7c):
For who is the son whom a father does not
   discipline?

Contrary (12:8):
If you are without formative discipline, of which
   all [children]
have become partakers, then you are bastards and
   not sons.

Comparison (12:9–10):
Since we have had our biological fathers as
   educators and showed reverence,
shall we not much more be subject to the Father
   of spirits and live?

Rationale (12:10):
For they disciplined us for a few days as seemed
   best to them,
but he [disciplines us] for our benefit, that we may
   share his holiness.

*Conclusion, incorporating a paraphrased quotation
of an authority* (12:11):
All formative discipline [*paideia*], while it is
   present, does not seem to be joyful, but grievous;
but later it yields the peaceful fruit [*karpon*] of
   righteousness to those who have been trained
   through it.[8]

---

8. Burton Mack (*Rhetoric*, 77–78) had correctly identified this passage as an example of the elaboration pattern, though he incorrectly
analyzed its constituent parts. In part, this was due to not giving proper
attention to the inferential particles in the text itself (e.g., the appear-
ance of the Greek word *gar*, "for," in 12:6, 10) and labeling 12:7c as an
argument from "example," whereas no actual argument from historical
example is employed in this passage. Hebrews 8:1–13 also resembles
this pattern, though with greater variation.

The author of Hebrews thus exhibits a clear knowledge and mastery of a preliminary pattern of rhetorical argumentation, using it with modest variation (for example, adding a rationale to the argument from comparison, a kind of variation allowed and modeled also in *Rhetorica ad Herennium*).

The preacher's conclusion (12:11)—truly a *piece de resistance* in terms of demonstrating textbook knowledge of argumentation—is an expanded paraphrase of a well-known maxim attributed sometimes to Isocrates, sometimes to Aristotle:[9] "the root of education ['discipline,' *paideia*] is bitter, but its fruit [*karpos*] is sweet." Hermogenes recites this maxim in his *Progymnasmata* and, in fact, uses it as *the chreia* around which he develops his sample elaboration (3.7). Learning how to paraphrase a *chreia* or maxim, both in abbreviated and expanded form, moreover, was itself an exercise included within the *Progymnasmata*. The first-century CE teacher Theon of Alexandria gives detailed attention to this exercise in his own *Prosgymnasmata*. The author of Hebrews exhibits precisely this learned technique in 12:11. Two key words from the well-known maxim—"discipline" (*paideia*) and "fruit" (*karpos*)—are preserved in the expanded form, and all of its other elements are represented somehow in the paraphrase.[10] The fact that the author concludes an argument constructed after a standard textbook pattern (the "elaboration" pattern) with a

9. Mack, *Rhetoric*, 78. Attridge (*Hebrews*, 364 n. 75) cites the version of this saying found in *Vit. phil.* 5.18, who attributes it to Aristotle.

10. The temporal relationship between enduring the rigors of education and enjoying its payoff represented by the metaphors of "root" and "fruit" in the original maxim are expressed explicitly in the temporal expressions "while it is present" and "but later"; the "bitterness" of discipline is captured in the phrase "does not seem to be joyful, but grievous"; the "sweetness" of the fruit is represented by the more precise description of the fruit as "peaceful" and productive of "righteousness."

standard *chreia* used in several *Progymnasmata* as the sample *chreia* on the basis of which the various exercises are demonstrated, artfully presenting this maxim in an expansive paraphrase such as the elementary exercises teach, compounds the impression that the author has received formal training in rhetoric at least at this secondary level.

The author of Hebrews evidences far more advanced facility in oratory than was associated with progymnastic training.[11] He skillfully uses argumentative topics familiar from deliberative oratory (speeches promoting acceptance or rejection of a particular course of action) and epideictic oratory (speeches amplifying the honor or disgrace of a particular person), and doing so in ways that do not become confused but are rather mutually supportive (hence the frequently observed alternation of "exposition" and "exhortation" throughout the sermon). He goes even further, however, in giving attention to rhetorical ornamentation and stylistic "polish." The opening sentence (1:1–4) evidences numerous skillfully employed rhetorical techniques already at work:

> In many and various ways God spoke of old to our fathers by the prophets; but in these last days he has spoken to us in a Son, whom he appointed the heir of all things, through whom also he created the world. He reflects the glory of God and bears the very stamp of his nature, upholding the universe by his word of power.

In the Greek, the opening twelve words greet the hearers with a striking use of alliteration, repeating the sound |p| five

---

11. See, further, deSilva, *Perseverance*, 37–58, and the literature discussed therein.

times.[12] The two parallel clauses in 1:3 employ the device of *homoeoteleuton*, ending with the same sounds and cadence (*-staseōs autou, -nameōs autou*).[13] Hebrews 1:1–2a shows perfect parallelism of the constituent clauses, developed by means of a complex antithesis (a set of contrasts):

"of old"	"to the ancestors"	"through the prophets"
"in these last days"	"to us"	"in a son"

In addition to judicious use of alliteration, Hebrews provides the most extended example of anaphora in the New Testament with the relentless repetition of "by faith" in chapter 11.[14] Such observations of rhetorical ornamentation can be made throughout the sermon, suggesting a studied rather than a casual acquaintance with the artistic use of language.[15]

CULTURAL LOCATION

The author is a Jewish Christian, most likely of Diaspora origin, and at least of Diaspora upbringing. He is expert in the Jewish Scriptures and in the science of their interpretation. He employs several interpretive techniques known from Jewish

12. Attridge cites the Greek text of 2:1–4; 4:16; 10:11, 34; 11:17; and 12:21 as other prominent examples of alliteration (*Hebrews*, 20 n. 157).

13. See Attridge, *Hebrews*, 20 nn. 145–47 for this and other indices of attention to rhythm in the author's prose composition. Aristotle advises: "prose must be rhythmical, but not metrical" (*Rhet.* 3.8.1, 3).

14. Cosby, *Rhetorical Composition*, 3; Kennedy, *New Testament Interpretation*, 156.

15. Attridge (*Hebrews*, 20–21) identifies several occurrences of assonance, asyndeton, brachylogy, chiasm, ellipse, hendiadys, hyperbaton, isocolon, litotes, and paronomasia (rhetorical figures discussed in book 4 of the *Rhet. Her.*; see also Trotter, *Interpreting the Epistle*, 163–80).

textbooks on the interpretation of Scripture, for example linking texts by a common key word to advance an interpretation, arguing from a lesser case to a weightier case (though this was also basic to Greco-Roman argumentation), and looking to the definitions of names and titles as keys to interpretation. In this single sermon he recites passages from Genesis, Exodus, Deuteronomy, 2 Samuel, multiple Psalms, Proverbs, Isaiah, Jeremiah, Haggai, and Habakkuk; he discusses several passages from Leviticus and Numbers in depth; and he alludes to stories and other material in the Pentateuch, Judges, Joshua, 1 and 2 Samuel, 1 and 2 Kings, Daniel, 2 Maccabees, and other traditions known now only from *Martyrdom of Isaiah* and *Lives of the Prophets*. He knows the whole of his sacred tradition, and he is able to deploy the whole of it to support his word of exhortation to this congregation. He reads these Scriptures, moreover, in the Greek translation in use among Greek-speaking Jews in the Western Diaspora (and Greek-speaking Jews resident in Palestine), a translation that would come to be known as the Septuagint. As is true for any translation, readings of the Scriptures in the Greek differ to some extent at many points from the readings of the same passages in the original Hebrew text. What is important here is that the author's recitations of Scripture often agree with known Greek texts of the Septuagint against known Hebrew texts of the same Scriptures.[16]

Alongside being fully immersed in the Scriptures of his own Jewish heritage, the author is also well acculturated to the Greco-Roman environment. In keeping with his own

16. This is most noticeably true at 1:6 (reciting Deut 32:43); 2:6–8 (reciting Ps 8:5–7); 3:7–11 (reciting Ps 95:7–11); 10:5–7 (reciting Ps 40:7–9); and 10:37–38 (reciting, rather loosely, Hab 2:3–4).

proximity to formal channels of education, he shares at least two fundamental tenets regarding education with his Greek cultural environment. The first emerges in his description of Jesus' own process of becoming qualified to serve as the perfect high priest, a process of formative education in which "he learned [*emathen*] obedience from the things he suffered [or 'experienced,' *epathen*]" (Heb 5:8). With the words "*ema-then . . . epathen*," the author incorporates a celebrated Greek wordplay, the classical equivalent of our "no pain, no gain."[17] Greek teachers sought to prepare their students to embrace the difficulties—even the pains—of the process of formative discipline (*paideia*) that would equip them with the skills, and carve into them the virtues, that would position them to flourish in Greek culture and leave behind a praiseworthy remembrance of a life well lived. Discipline did not merely involve punishment for doing something wrong (with the result that learning came from trial, error, and a whooping). Educative discipline challenged students with rigorous exercises training mind, soul, and body.

When the author describes the addressees' experiences of hardship as instances of divine discipline intended to strengthen their commitment and shape their character, though his launching-off point is a recitation of Proverbs 3:11–12, his discussion has much more in common with Seneca's essay *On Providence* (*Prov.*). Seneca describes the sage as God's "pupil, imitator and true progeny, whom that magnificent parent, no mild enforcer of virtues, educates quite sternly, just as strict fathers do" (*Prov.* 1.6). God "raises"

17. See, for example, Aeschylus, *Ag.* 177; Herodotus, *Hist.* 1.207. For further references, see Attridge, *Hebrews*, 152 n. 192; Croy, *Endurance*, 139–44.

or "brings up" the wise person like a son or daughter (2.5), and "tests, hardens, and prepares" the wise person to be God's own (1.6).[18] Seneca affirms that "those whom God approves and loves, God toughens, examines, and exercises" (4.7).[19] By means of these hardships, God prepares the disciple or sage for some greater destiny (described as "God's own self" in *On Providence*, and "a share in God's holiness" in Heb 12:10). Being subject to hardship shows that one is God's "true progeny" (*Prov.* 1.6), God's legitimate offspring rather than the contrary (see Heb 12:8). This remarkable Latin text suggests that the author of Hebrews, with his argument in 12:5–11, would have been as much at home in Seneca's parlor as in the Hellenistic synagogue.

The second tenet shared by the author of Hebrews with the Greek culture concerns the notion of discrete stages of instruction, with the student moving (ideally) from one to the next at the proper age. The author of Hebrews evokes this topic in a passage upbraiding the hearers for not having made greater progress in their formation as Christian disciples and not having made a surer transition to becoming themselves promoters and teachers of the Christian philosophy:

> You have become sluggish in hearing. For indeed, though you ought to be teachers on account of the amount of time that has elapsed, you again have need for someone to continue to teach you the most basic principles of the primary level of the oracles of God. You have come to stand in need of milk rather than solid food, for everyone who partakes of milk is unskilled in the word of righteousness, for he or she is an infant. But solid food is for the

18. Croy, *Endurance*, 149.
19. Ibid., 150.

mature, who have their faculties trained through
constant practice for the discernment of the noble
and the base. (5:11–14)

As the author attempts to shame the hearers into taking
a more active stance in regard to their own and one another's
formation, he employs common metaphors for levels of education to drive his appeal home. Milk versus meat, the infant
versus the mature adult, were frequently used by philosophers
to speak of stages of education or achievement in philosophy,
and often specifically in order to motivate greater progress
among the hearers in regard to their commitment to the philosophy's way of life and their internalization of its values.[20]

When the author describes the mature believer as one
who is equipped for "the discernment of what is noble and
what is wicked" (5:14), he incorporates a standard Greco-
Roman definition of the virtue of Wisdom, one of the four
cardinal virtues promoted by Platonists and Stoics and a feature of the mainstream of dominant cultural ethics. The mature person who has made sufficient progress in the formative
discipline offered by the "school" has attained wisdom: he or
she has "intelligence capable, by a certain judicious method,
of distinguishing good and bad" (*Rhet. Her.* 3.3.4–5).[21] In con-

20. See, for example, Epictetus, *Diss.* 2.16.39; 3.24.9 on milk; Seneca,
Ep. 88.20 on "elementary teachings"; Epictetus, *Diss.* 1.26.3; 2.18.27; and
Philo, *Virt.* 18 on education in the philosophy as "training." Paul also
makes use of these metaphors in 1 Cor 3:1–3, again in an effort to shame
the audience out of some failure to measure up to the expectations or
virtues of the Christian culture. On the cultural intertexture of philosophical texts and educational metaphors, see Thompson, *Beginnings*,
29–30; Attridge, *Hebrews*, 158–61.

21. Aristotle (*Rhet.* 1.9.13) similarly defines wisdom as an intellectual capacity for deliberating well about good and bad, thus moving
even closer to the decision-making function of wisdom.

text, the author draws on intertexture from the Greek cultural environment, rather than from the inherited tradition of the Jewish and Christian culture, to arouse the hearers' attention and shame them for not yet adequately exercising this faculty of wisdom and zealously encouraging and teaching one another about the truly advantageous course (namely, perseverance in association with the Christian minority group).[22]

The author of Hebrews includes some striking athletic imagery in his sermon. It is important to remember that the world of Greek games was closely related to the arena of Greek education, the *lyceum* and *gymnasium* being twin institutions serving the formative task of education (*paideia*). The most notable instance occurs at the climax of the celebration of the exemplars of faith (11:1—12:4):

> Having, therefore, such a great cloud of spectators surrounding us, let us also run with endurance the racecourse laid out before us, putting off every weight and the sin which so easily trips us up, looking away to faith's pioneer and perfecter—Jesus, who, for the sake of the joy set before him, endured a cross, despising shame, and has sat down at the right hand of God's throne. Consider him who had endured from sinners such hostility against himself, in order that you may not become faint, growing weary in your souls. You have not yet, while

22. I use the term "minority group" or "minority culture" here to label a social body in contrast to "dominant culture" and "majority culture," embracing a variety of non-dominant, non-majority cultures (sub-cultures, counter-cultures, contra-cultures). The terminology comes from an article seeking to provide a more precise language for the social relationships between, and social location of, particular groups within a multi-cultural context where different groups have varying access to power (K. Roberts, "Toward a Generic Concept").

> contending in the ring against sin, fought back to
> the point of spilling your own blood (12:1–4).

The author brings together the two events of running and wrestling, both major focal points for training and competition in Greek games, in a manner showing some familiarity with the events. He first directs attention to the stands of the stadium, filled with a particular quality of spectators of the events in which the audience will compete.[23] He uses a "fixed classical expression" to describe a race the course of which is determined by the masters of the games ("the course laid out before us," *ton prokeimenon hēmin agōna*).[24] He draws attention to the need for the appropriate state of dress (or undress, as the case may be). And, like a good coach, he keeps his runners' minds fixed on the best example of how to run this race course well, so that his exemplar's strategies, skills, and success will empower their own running. He shifts metaphors in 12:4 from the racetrack to the wrestling floor, where each believer is pitted against "Sin," the antagonist whom they must defeat. The athletic metaphor enters the text again in 12:11 with the word "training" (*gegymnasmenois*), a

23. This usage of *martys* is well attested in contemporary Greek literature. Wisdom 1:6 speaks of God as "a witness [*martys*] of the inmost feelings, a true observer of their hearts and a hearer of their tongues." The parallelism shows "witness" to be used here in the sense of "onlooker/observer." Josephus uses the term to speak of people observing acts of courage or moral failure, who will thence attest to the subject's honor or worthlessness (see *B.J.* 4.134 and *Ant.* 18.299). The first three texts are listed in Attridge, *Hebrews*, 354 n. 19 and are developed in greater detail in Croy, *Endurance*, 58–61.

24. Attridge (*Hebrews*, 355) refers to Euripides, *Orest.* 847; Plato, *Laches* 182A; Epictetus, *Diss.* 3.25.3; Josephus, *Ant.* 19.1.13 §92. Croy (*Endurance*, 66) adds Plato, *Phaedr.* 247b; Dio, *Or.* 13.118.

verbal echo of the *gymnasion* ("gymnasium") where the future citizens of the Greek city-state trained for the development of physical prowess and strength as part of the larger process of *paideia*, now used to speak of God's training of the disciples for the formation of the virtues of justice and holiness. Once again, the specific use to which the author puts the imagery shows his own proximity to Greek and Roman philosophical culture, cultural knowledge most likely acquired via channels of a Judaism that was itself highly influenced by Greek culture (for example, the culture of Philo and the author of 4 Maccabees).[25] In these circles, athletic imagery was used to interpret the experiences of hardship that frequently accompanied the pursuit of the school's philosophical ideals, to encourage ongoing endurance toward the goals espoused by the group in face of ongoing hardship.[26]

The author's acquaintance with Greco-Roman philosophy emerges also in his summary of what the example of Jesus, the founder of the Christian "philosophy," taught his followers:

> Since, then, the children have shared flesh and blood in common, he himself also fully shared the same things in order that, through death, he might destroy the one holding the power of death, namely the Slanderer, and set free those who were

25. For more detailed discussion, see Pfitzner, *Paul and the Agon Motif*; Croy, *Endurance*, 37–77, 167–82; deSilva, *Perseverance*, 361–64, 426–30.

26. See 4 Macc 5:16; 7:4 9:18, 30; 11:20–21; Epictetus, *Diss.* 3.24.71; 4.1.60, 87; Philo, *Prob.* 29–30; Seneca, *Constant.* 5.6–7; 9.5. Further uses of athletic imagery can be observed in Seneca, *Prov.* 2.3–4; Epictetus, *Diss.* 1.18.21; 1.24.1–2; 3.20.9; 3.22.52, 56; Dio, *Or.* 8.11–16; 4 Macc 16:16; 17:11–16.

liable to slavery all their lives by the fear of death.
(Heb 2:14–15)

Jesus is celebrated for having brought an enormous benefit to humankind—at least, to those who would internalize the lesson of his own life—liberating them from the power of death (through our fear of death as mortals) to constrain our wills and imaginations. While this passage resonates with Jewish apocalyptic traditions of the Messiah's victory over demonic forces,[27] it also draws upon Greek philosophical discourse on being set free from the fear of death by the courageous example of key teachers facing their own deaths. The author presents Jesus in a manner reminiscent of Seneca's portrayal of Socrates (*Ep.* 24.4): "Socrates in prison . . . declined to flee when certain persons gave him the opportunity . . . in order to free humankind from the fear of two most grievous things, death and imprisonment." In the early second century CE, a wandering sophist named Peregrinus imitated Socrates's pattern for the sake of teaching his followers a similar lesson by burning himself to death upon a pyre (and, according to the cynical Lucian, securing his own reputation as a genuine philosopher after a less-than-illustrious career): "[Peregrinus] alleges that he is doing it . . . that he may teach them to despise death and endure what is fearsome" (Lucian, *Peregr.* 23; see also *Peregr.* 33). The author of Hebrews sounds very "Greek," then, as he attributes to Jesus the freedom from the fear of death that enabled him to maintain his own virtue intact in the face of opposition and suffering, thus becoming a model enabling his followers to maintain their virtuous

27. See Attridge, *Hebrews*, 93 n. 153 for comparative texts.

response to God no matter what society might seek to do to hinder them.[28]

The author emerges, then, from Greek-speaking Judaism, and a Judaism that is very much open to the insights of Greek philosophical culture and to education in Greek language and rhetoric. It is important to distinguish carefully, however, between acculturation and the uses to which a particular author puts acculturation when assessing social location. As we will see in the chapters that follow, the author uses his facility in Greek language, rhetoric, and philosophical discourse to encourage other members of the Christian minority culture to maintain their stance of critical distance from both the synagogue and the Greco-Roman society, particularly where participation in worship is concerned. He does not use his cultural knowledge to encourage "rapprochement" between the Christians and their neighbors but, in fact, to promote the group's social distance and distinctiveness—to reinforce their willingness to continue to live in the margins of society rather than move back toward its centers.

AUTHORITY

A basic set of sociological questions concerns the distribution of power and the authority relations at work between parties in a particular group. In every system there will be an unequal

28. Ronald Williamson ("Platonism and Hebrews") and Lincoln Hurst (*Background*, 7–42) have also drawn attention to the author's awareness of Platonic terms, for example "type" and "shadow" (8:5; 10:1), as mediated through Hellenistic Jewish philosophy as evidence of the author's cultural location. While their observations are correct, the author of Hebrews also maintains a thoroughly apocalyptic worldview (see deSilva, *Perseverance*, 27–32) and, in this important regard, stands alongside Paul and against Philo and Plato.

distribution of power: some members will have more "voice" than others. Even in a community that seeks to be egalitarian, those who found the community will inevitably have more power, even if this is exerted only in the ways in which their initial vision and interactions create a culture into which others will be invited and socialized, with the culture thus exercising "constraints" upon the converts. This fact raises the question of "legitimate authority": what makes the unequal distribution of power in a system (whether a family, a voluntary organization, a city, a nation) acceptable, or essentially acceptable, to all parties? What gives one person the "right" to constrain another person's choices and behavior in some way, such that the latter person accepts the constraints?

Pioneering sociologist Max Weber distinguished three basic types of basis for "legitimate authority," that is, for authority that is granted to a figure or figures by subordinates on this basis.[29] His catalog would not be applicable to situations of coercive domination, where force is the guarantor of power and acquiescence (though it is admittedly the *final* guarantor of power in many situations where authority is otherwise generally accepted as legitimate), nor to situations of negotiated domination, where mutual self-interest is the final reason for according authority. Legitimation of authority is especially important in voluntary associations such as the early church—that is, where there is indeed no recourse to force should a leader's authority be rejected.

The first type of authority is "charismatic" authority, based in the authority figure's supposed nearness to the sources of divine or other superhuman, supernatural power and presence, or his or her otherwise extraordinary character

29. Weber, "Three Types"; idem, *Economy and Society*, 215.

or heroism, or his or her extraordinary ability to give voice and direction to the deepest aspirations of the audience that gathers around him or her. Jesus certainly is accorded, and exercises, authority on this basis: his miracles, his confrontation of evil supernatural forces, his aura of awareness of the divine presence all combined to impress upon onlookers his distinctive connection with God and, on that basis, his authorization upon earth to speak for God and to be heeded.

The second type is "traditional" legitimation. A person has authority because people in his or her family have always had authority (as is the case in hereditary monarchies), or because he or she enacts a role that has been vested with authority (as in the case of fathers in patriarchal or mothers in matriarchal societies).

The third type is "rational-legal" legitimation, in which a person's authority is carefully specified in terms of the office that he or she occupies in the context of a well-developed bureaucracy, and in which a person rises to authority and exercises authority in keeping with those rules. Judges and bishops are granted authority on this basis, in keeping with the principles upon which their offices are established. A corrupt judge or an illegally elected bishop will lose legitimacy as an authority figure.

To distinguish these types another way, where authority is granted on the basis of charisma, people give their allegiance to an individual; where authority is granted on traditional grounds, people give their allegiance to an established system; where authority is granted on legal-rational grounds, people give their allegiance to a set of principles. In real-life situations, these types are often mixed, and they are also not exhaustive.[30]

In the sociology of the early Christian movement, Jesus would be seen as the charismatic founder. According to the fundamental convictions of the group, Jesus may have been removed from everyday access but he was never ultimately removed from the headship of the movement, continuing to guide and empower from his place at God's right hand (see, for example, Heb 1:3, 13; 8:1; 10:12). What this means is that the institutionalized means of access to the leader's guidance and empowerment become infused with derived authority. The message of and about the absent leader, however this is accessed (in the traditions of Jesus' sayings, in ways of reading the sacred Scriptures, in communications to, about, or even *from* the absent leader, in the community itself as a place where people "draw near" to Jesus and experience his presence and the access to the divine that he provides) continues to have primary authority.

In Jesus' absence, his closest followers (the inner circle of "apostles") become the primary, functional leaders of the movement. They are his "staff," directly commissioned by the charismatic leader, possessing a derived charisma from their proximity to him. They are charged with carrying on the leader's message and mission, which becomes "institutionalized" in sayings traditions, summary formulas, traditions of interpreting sacred texts, ways of "being together" in communities

30. For example, a person can be accorded authority because he or she gets the job done, or because of his or her accomplishments in the past, which bode well for effective leadership in the present. This could be termed "functional legitimation," and Paul seems to appeal to it on occasion (see 1 Cor 4:15; 15:10).

of Christ-followers, and cultic rites. Paul enters this circle of apostles in an irregular manner, directly commissioned by the charismatic leader but not through connection with Jesus in his earthly work. He acts as a kind of charismatic entrepreneur himself, forming communities with close personal bonds of allegiance to himself, but always on behalf of and self-consciously subordinate to the ultimate leader of the movement, Jesus.[31] It is significant that Paul's acceptance within and by the older circle of apostles is a topic of discussion (see, for example, Gal 2:1–14); even if he would deny it, it appears that he needs their acknowledgment, as those with closer and more easily demonstrated connections with the fount of charisma (Jesus), for his ministry to be effective.

Paul works as part of a larger mission, having both partners (like Barnabas and Apollos, who are not subordinate to Paul) and staff (like Timothy and Titus, who are invited into the work of the mission by Paul). Such people are in closer proximity to the point of origin of the movement than the typical convert, and are thus in a direct position to cooperate together in giving shape to the movement as they participate in the planting and nurture of new churches and exercise ongoing authority over those communities. Finally, leaders also emerge within the local churches. These are likely people who were among the first converts in a given location, who thereby become an important circle supporting the continuing growth of the new community by providing hospitality for the apostle and for the gathered converts and other material support, who participate in giving specific shape to the community in that locale, and upon whom the apostle can rely to continue to preserve the work in his or her absence.

31. Holmberg, *Paul and Power*, 157.

On what basis, then, does the author of Hebrews ask that his authority to speak to and direct the audience in their situation be recognized? Or in other words, why does the audience listen to this speaker and entertain the possibility that what he has to say should impact what they do in and with their lives, potentially at significant cost to themselves?

One avenue for answering this question would be to locate the author in the chain leading to the formation of the community he addresses. He does not present himself as a personal witness of the Lord Jesus, but rather as one who has himself been evangelized by those who were Jesus' witnesses (Heb 2:3). He thus does not exercise authority on the same basis as the community's founder or founders, whether this was Paul himself or another member of the Christian mission sympathetic to Paul and his view concerning the inclusion of Gentiles. The author is also not a leader from within the community to which he writes, for he always refers to this circle of local leaders in the third person (13:7, 17, 24). He does, however, write in support of the local leadership and therefore, perhaps, stands in some ways above it, continuing to authorize it by his own endorsement.

The author often associates himself with the audience as a collective "we" or "us," to which his statements about God's actions on their behalf, their collective identity in Christ, and their obligations to God and to one another apply equally. That is, at many points he speaks of himself, his circle, and his audience as standing alike and equally under the sacred message of Jesus and its associated obligations.[32] But at one point (4:1)

32. See Heb 1:2a; 2:1–3, 8–9; 3:6, 14; 4:2–3, 13–16; 6:1–2; 7:19, 26; 8:1; 9:14, 24; 10:15, 19–24, 26, 30, 39; 11:3, 40; 12:1–2, 9, 25b–29; 13:13–15.

he begins to differentiate pointedly between what is applicable to this collective "we" and what is applicable only to the "you" or individual members of the "you" of the audience. In a few passages (5:11–12; 6:9–12; 13:18) he identifies himself as part of a "we" that is clearly distinct from and does not include the "you" of the audience, a "we" that is set over the audience and in a position either to affirm or censure their behavior. From this standpoint, the author can issue commands and speak directly to this audience (e.g., 3:1, 12–13; 10:32–36; 12:3–8, 12–17, 25; 13:2–7, 9, 16–17, 18, 22–25). He emerges as a distinct "I" at only a few places (11:32; 13:19, 22–23).

The author hereby locates himself within the circle of those responsible for the conversion and nurture of the recipients in Christian faith and practice. He has visited the community before, since he hopes to be "restored" to them (13:19). He is part of a group, including Timothy (a deeply rooted member of the Pauline mission team, 13:23), that does not belong to any one congregation but, rather, exercises oversight across a wider region that includes many congregations as the staff of the founder or founders of those congregations. They are therefore structurally closer to the originating point of the movement, above the jurisdiction of any local congregation, with many local congregations falling under their jurisdiction as they carry on the work of the absent apostle (whether Paul moved on to new mission grounds or died). Addressing a letter of instruction to (and, similarly, visiting) a congregation enacts an established pattern among members of this group as an act of oversight,[33] and the pattern itself

33. On the establishment and enacting of "roles" as a primary expression of institutionalization, see Holmberg, *Paul and Power*, 166–67; Berger and Luckmann, *Social Construction*, 73.

carries with it the expectation—on the author's part *and* on the audience's part—that the message bears authority.

With the sermon itself, the author does not rely on purely charismatic legitimation, claiming to have received his words as special revelations from God or to stand closer to God's power and favor than the recipients, such that he mediates the same on their behalf (see again, in this regard, 2:3–4). He does not make explicit claims concerning his authorization by the senior apostle, hence on a kind of primitive "charter" for his right to be heeded. Instead, from beginning to end, he relies on his ability to connect his exhortations with the authoritative traditions of the community (chiefly the Old Testament and the proclamation of Jesus). He depends upon the community's allegiance to those Scriptures and that proclamation, and, indeed, to the relationship with the living Lord formed as a result of their conversion. He asks to be heard to the extent that he represents that tradition and speaks in line with and on behalf of that tradition. He implicitly claims to understand the implications of the tradition and the divine-human relationship forged in Christ better than some of the recipients, for he repeatedly chides them for not living up to the same. In this sense, he presents himself as standing closer to the underlying "sacred *ratio*," the knowledge about God and the world shared by the group and standing at the heart of the community's historical existence as a distinct group, and claims the right to direct the community's steps on this basis.[34]

Fundamental to the shared knowledge between the author and the members of early Christian congregations is

34. "The really crucial form of proximity to the sacred is that of being in contact with sacred *ratio*, the divine Word: apostles, prophets and teachers are the real 'authorities' during the first years of the Church" (Holmberg, *Paul and Power*, 195–96; see also 132–33).

the conviction that God has "spoken in the prophets" (1:1) and that the divine voice remains accessible in the Scriptures, which the author of Hebrews calls "the oracles of God" (5:12). The author grounds his own address fully in the text of these "oracles of God" and, more specifically, in the Christ-centered interpretation of the same, around which these same early Christian communities were formed. His sermon opens by amplifying the honor and gravity of the Son of God (1:1–14) and, thereby, amplifying the weight or seriousness of the word spoken in, by, and about this Son and the obligation to respond appropriately to this word (2:1–4). Because it *is* God's voice that is heard in the proclamation made by Jesus (2:3a), and now in the proclamation made about Jesus' death and resurrection and its import for human beings by Jesus' witnesses (2:3b), "it is necessary to pay close attention" to the message around which the church was formed (2:1), and to which God himself bore witness in the initial proclamation of the same (2:4).

Insofar as the author draws from beginning to end on the sacred "oracles of God," the audience might legitimately wonder who is speaking throughout Hebrews. At many points, it is explicitly God, or the Son, or the Spirit speaking (1:5, 6, 7, 13; 2:12–13; 3:7–11; 4:3–4; 5:5–6; 6:14; 7:21; 8:8; 10:5, 15, 30; 12:25, 26; 13:5), as the author attributes recitations from the sacred Scriptures to one of these spokespersons of the divine voice. Indeed, in his repeated recitation of Ps 95:7 ("Today if you hear his voice, do not harden your hearts," in Heb 3:7, 15; 4:7) the author leads the audience to listen with the expectation that they will hear the divine voice speaking to them through it. The author's challenge potentially becomes God's challenge, and the audience will potentially respond to the author's sermon as to the divine voice itself (see also 12:25), and the audience is positioned to respond more readily to the author's challenge by the threat of refusing to heed the divine voice potentially speaking therein.

The re-proclamation of this message and the delineation of the appropriate response to that message in Hebrews, therefore, is invested with divine authority insofar as the audience discerns in it a faithful re-presentation and development of the sacred *ratio* that stands at the root of the group's formation. To the extent that the author is successful in this alignment, his speech will impose constraints on the audience's choices and actions (or force them consciously to abandon the group and reject its sacred *ratio*). Without claiming any special divine commission, prophetic words from the Lord, or visions of the realm beyond the visible, then, the author is able to claim divine authorization for his message and to open the audience's eyes to vistas beyond the visible realm (e.g., the activity of Jesus as the high priest of the heavenly Holy Place, 9:11—10:18), all on the basis of the interpretation of texts held as sacred and authoritative jointly by author and audience. His rhetorical ability,[35] which distinguishes him above his canonical peers, no doubt also contributed greatly to his authority, as virtuosity as a speaker was an important ingredient of authority in the first-century Greco-Roman environment. The preservation and eventual canonization of the sermon despite persistent questions about its authorship testifies to the widespread reception of this author's address as, indeed, a faithful representation of the divine Word speaking to the early church's contexts.

35. See deSilva, *Perseverance*, 35–39, 46–58.

TWO

The Audience of Hebrews: A Social Profile

LOCATION, ETHNICITY, AND SOCIAL LEVEL

Social-scientific exploration of Hebrews is rendered more challenging insofar as the text itself is silent not only on the identity of the author, but also the location of the addressees. One reason that the Corinthian Correspondence has been such a fruitful collection of texts for sociological analysis is that it locates the audience firmly and indisputably in first-century Roman Corinth, a city that has been well excavated, whose social structures and civic life are well documented in surviving inscriptions, and about which there are significant ancient literary records.[1] All of these sources have much to contribute to the study of the social setting of the Christian congregations

---

1. Excellent examples include Theissen, *Pauline Christianity*; Meeks, *First Urban Christians*; de Vos, *Church and Community Conflicts*; Horrell, *Social Ethos*.

taking shape in Corinth and the relationship between this context and the issues that arise within the group.[2]

If the author of Hebrews had begun his communication using the standard opening for a letter that is common among New Testament writings rather than in a manner appropriate for a sermon or oration, we would have recourse to this kind of information as we develop a social profile for the audience and look for the correlations between the audience's situation and the author's textual strategy. The only certain geographical reference point we have comes in the letter's closing: "those from Italy greet you" (13:24). Some read this as an indication that the author is sending greetings back *to* Italy from those now separated from their sisters and brothers, and thus that he addresses Christian communities in Italy, most likely Rome.[3] However, the expression may equally well indicate that the author, writing *from* Italy, is sending greetings from his compatriots to a church located outside of Italy.[4] Early scribes attempted to clarify the setting

2. There is some discussion in scholarship concerning the propriety of calling first-century Christ-followers "Christians." The label was, however, clearly applied to followers of Jesus as Messiah in late-first and early-second-century texts from within and outside the group (see Acts 11:26; 26:28; 1 Pet 4:16; Tacitus, *Ann.* 15.44; Pliny, *Ep.* 10.96). The author of Acts speaks of the term being applied *de novo* to followers of Jesus in Antioch even before the outset of Paul's missionary travels (11:26). I therefore conclude that it is not inappropriate for modern scholars to continue to use the term "Christian" to designate the avidly proselytizing Jewish messianic sect that claimed allegiance to Jesus. I use the term as I might apply the label "Pharisee," "Essene," or "Sadducee" to other Jewish groups clearly discernible against the larger landscape of Jews who did not differentiate themselves from other Jews with any such labels.

3. Lane, *Hebrews 1–8*, lviii; Pfitzner, *Hebrews*, 30.

4. Attridge (*Hebrews*, 410 n. 79) provides a list of texts where the expression indicates place of origin, rather than separation from a place.

by adding a line at the sermon's close about the who, whence, and whither:

> "To the Hebrews, written from Rome"
>
> "To the Hebrews, written from Italy"
>
> "To the Hebrews, written from Italy through Timothy"
>
> "To the Hebrews, written from Rome by Paul to those in Jerusalem"
>
> "To the Hebrews, written in Hebrew from Italy anonymously through Timothy"

What is immediately clear is that these scribes had no more data on which to base their judgments than we do. It is noteworthy that those scribes who do comment on 13:24 unanimously read this as an indication that the text was sent *from* Rome or Italy to some other destination, and not that the letter was written *to* Christians at Rome, against trends in modern scholarship.[5]

Scholars must choose between wedding their reading to a specific geographical location that remains, however, conjectural and conducting their analysis of the audience and its situation on the basis of the internal evidence provided by the text itself. Many scholars, like the early scribes, opt for the former. The most popular conjecture, of course, is a Roman Christian

---

5. Thus manuscripts A, P, 739, 1881, 81 (to Jerusalem!), 104, and 0285. The conjecture that the letter was written "through Timothy" appears to be an incorrect inference from Heb 13:23. Timothy is not present with the writer at the time of composition, and so could not have been instrumental in its composition. The author also plans to visit the congregation *with* Timothy, if he shows up, not send the letter by means of Timothy.

audience, and the occasion is often bound somehow with Nero's persecution of the Roman Christian communities.[6]

6. Correlations between Hebrews and 1 Peter (written from Rome to churches throughout Asia Minor) do not advance the case that Hebrews was written to Rome (vs. Attridge, *Hebrews*, 10). The similarities in the situations addressed by Hebrews and 1 Peter suggest, rather, that a Christian teacher in Rome is writing to a church in one of the provinces for which he feels a special pastoral responsibility. Lane (*Hebrews 1–9*, lviii–lxvi) provides the most detailed argument in favor of locating the addressees in Rome, leading to a highly specified reconstruction of the community's history and present setting on the eve of the Neronian persecution.

Ellen Aitken ("Portraying the Temple," 137–44) illumines the presence of motifs of the Roman triumph in the author of Hebrews' presentation of Jesus' return to the heavenly realm, and demonstrates that the images of Jesus' triumph in Hebrews would have been especially poignant if read in the social context of Rome under the Flavians (and perhaps most poignant after the erection of the Arch of Titus by Domitian), when the Flavian triumph over Judea and its temple were prominent features of the ongoing legitimation of the new dynasty. To demonstrate that a work would have been poignant *in* a particular situation, however, is not to demonstrate that it was actually written *for* that situation. The imagery of the Roman triumph was available to the author of Hebrews at any point after the death of Jesus (and speaks once again more to the author's location in Rome rather than the audience's). The apotheosis of the deceased emperor was also available as a foil for the ascension and enthronement of the true Son of God (the *filius dei* rather than the *filius divi*) from the beginning of the principate.

Aitken ("Portraying the Temple," 134) reads Heb 10:32–34 as a reminiscence of the Neronian persecution, but when compared with Tacitus, *Ann.* 15.44, Hebrews seems to be addressing a community that has experienced far less dire circumstances. Indeed, Heb 12:4 specifically denies the occurrence of martyrdom within the community addressed. Even if this does not prove that *no* Christians around them had been martyred, the author's silence about any Christian martyrs (all the more when he is attuned to the Maccabean martyrs and the martyred prophets) is difficult to explain if Nero's persecution has already occurred in Rome (*if* the audience is indeed in Rome).

However, some have proposed (on the basis of the alleged similarities between Hebrews and the "Colossian heresy") that Hebrews was written for Christians in the churches of the Lycus Valley.[7] Several scholars, following the lead of a single ancient conjecture, have suggested that the sermon was written to Christians in Jerusalem itself, perhaps to pilgrims who had arrived too late to witness Jesus' ministry but were converted soon thereafter and encouraged to persevere.[8] None of these settings is impossible, though some are far more plausible than others. I prefer, however, to remain agnostic on the question of destination and, therefore, limit the extent to which I will admit external (and potentially irrelevant, even misleading) data to our analysis of the audience's situation and the author's diagnosis and interpretation of their condition.

The title traditionally ascribed to this sermon—evidenced in manuscripts of the New Testament writings at least as early as the late second century CE—has exercised undue prejudice on reconstructions of the audience's social profile. The consequences of this prejudice are seen already in those manuscripts that claim the work to have been written "to those in Jerusalem" or even "*in* Hebrew." But the title "To the Hebrews" is a second-century conjecture about the original audience based on the copyists' observations about its content, namely its interest in Jewish rites and scriptures.[9] Second-century Christians might have tended to view this letter as addressing Christian *Jews* precisely because the Christian group needed

7. Jewett, *Letter to Pilgrims*, 5–7.

8. See Buchanan, *To The Hebrews*; Gleason, "Old Testament Background."

9. The person "who attached a title to this document . . . was probably just speculating about its original recipients and was as much in the dark as we are" (Long, *Hebrews*, 1).

some kind of canonical "response" to the parent religion that had rejected them, a manifesto of the superiority of Jesus and the movement formed in his name to the parent religion.

In support of this traditional conjecture about the intended audience, one commonly encounters several assumptions. First, it is alleged that the extensive use of the Old Testament (the Jewish Scriptures) presumes a Jewish-Christian audience. However, texts like Galatians and 1 Peter, both of which are clearly addressed to Gentile Christians (no doubt with some number of Jewish Christians in their midst), show us that Gentile Christians would be assumed to be highly interested in, and able to follow, arguments based on the Jewish Scriptures. These texts also demonstrate that Gentile Christians would specifically be interested in how those Scriptures could illumine their standing within a covenant relationship made between God and a particular (Jewish) people and their relationship to the particular institutions found within Israel, the historic people of God. Every New Testament letter bears witness to its author's assumption that *Gentile* Christians also received the *Jewish* Scriptures as the "oracles of God" (indeed, as their inheritance by virtue of being joined to the "true Israel").[10]

A second assumption is that Gentile Christians would not be interested in Jewish cult (or its implications for thinking about Jesus' death),[11] and that attempts to prove the ob-

10. See Moffatt, *Hebrews*, xvi–xvii: "how much the LXX meant to Gentile Christians may be seen in the case of a man like Tatian, for example, who explicitly declares that he owed to reading of the OT his conversion to Christianity (*Ad Graecos*, 29)." Justin Martyr (*Dial.* 8) has a similar testimony.

11. Ellingworth (*Hebrews*, 25), for example, thinks that the author's interest in the Jewish cult "would probably have left gentile readers cold."

solescence of the Old Covenant (such as one finds in Heb 7:1—10:18, and especially 8:1–13) are a matter of importance for Jewish, but not Gentile, Christians.[12] This assumption, like the former, does not take sufficiently seriously the fact that Gentile Christians, by virtue of their conversion, received the Jewish Scriptures as divine revelation. The sermon "to the Hebrews" directly addresses a major scandal of the Old Testament for Gentile Christian adherents, namely the particular challenge of how to read the Old Testament as a record of divine revelation while rejecting the sacrificial system and cultic regulations commanded therein.

A third assumption, following from the first two, is that the presenting issue is the danger of a *return* to Judaism and relating to God through the temple worship service on the part of Jewish Christians on account of the latter's desire to avoid ongoing tension with their non-Christian Jewish families and neighbors.[13] The lengthy argument in Heb 7:1—10:18 concerning the Levitical cult, however, does not necessarily presuppose a return to temple worship as the pressing problem among the addressees. Rather, it serves the positive goal of affirming for all Christians that they stand in the more privileged position in the history of God's experience with humanity, which will, in turn, sustain commitment to Christ and forestall apostasy in any direction (whether toward pagan religion or non-Christian Jewish practice). Reading Hebrews as if it addressed a primarily Jewish Christian audience, moreover, has tended to prevent readers from perceiving how the sustained comparison of Jesus with the mediators of

12. Gleason, "Old Testament Background," 67.

13. Peterson, *Hebrews and Perfection*, 186; Hughes, *Hebrews*, 18–19; Gleason, "Old Testament Background," 69.

access to God under the Torah and Levitical cult contributed positively to the formation of Christian identity, rather than merely serve as a series of polemics against an alleged "reversion" to Judaism. Moreover, we have no firm indication that Jewish Christians as a rule *ceased* to participate in the temple cult prior to 70 CE, either in person or through the payment of the temple tax, and Matt 17:24–27 is a positive indication to the contrary.

No internal evidence, then, points to a Jewish Christian audience *as opposed to* a Gentile Christian audience. The language of the sermon and the author's familiarity with and reliance on the Greek translation of the Jewish Scriptures (rather than a known Hebrew textual tradition, as one finds in James and Jude) seriously undermine the appropriateness of the title "To the Hebrews," at least in relation to the traditional distinction between Hebrews and Hellenists in the early church (as in Acts 6:1–6). But there are two positive indications of Gentile Christians included among the audience. First, in Heb 6:1–2, the author refers to a catechism of topics that would be familiar already to Jewish converts, but which would be important to introduce to Gentile converts. Second, the mention of Timothy and inclusion of the same in the author's travel plans (13:23) strongly suggests that the particular congregation addressed was formed as part of the Pauline mission. This mission had as its explicit goal the raising up of Gentile Christians and forming mixed communities of Gentile Christians and Hellenistic Jewish Christians, hence the history of Paul's confrontations with James, the Judaizers, and other Jewish Christians like Peter and Barnabas in Antioch. It seems prudent, therefore, not to allow the secondary title to obscure the likelihood that the author addresses a mixed congregation of Jewish and Gentile Christians.[14]

One other typical concern of social-scientific inquiry involves the social level of the members of a particular group. Hebrews provides further evidence against the older, Marxian assumption that early Christianity recruited "mainly from the labouring and burdened, the members of the lowest strata of the people," consisting of "slaves and emancipated slaves, of poor people deprived of all rights."[15] Linguistically, Hebrews is composed in very stylish and difficult Greek. The author uses extensive and rare vocabulary (Hebrews has the highest number of words occurring only once in the New Testament of all New Testament writers). He writes in a somewhat classical style, and his syntax is more complex (more independent of word order) than one finds in other New Testament texts. This already suggests an audience capable of attending to such language and syntax, unless the author was simply a bad preacher who spoke over the heads of his congregation. The author, however, also tells us that some members of the community possessed property worth confiscating (10:34). Some were (and continue to be) capable of charitable activity in the community and of showing hospitality to visiting Christian travelers (13:2; 10:33b–34a; 13:16). The author warns against over-ambition, both with regard to possessions (13:5) and status (13:14), warnings that apply more to "haves" than "have-nots." Not all members of the audience, then, came

14. Attridge, *Hebrews*, 10–13; Eisenbaum, *Jewish Heroes*, 8–9; deSilva, *Perseverance*, 2–7.

15. Marx and Engels, *On Religion*, 316, 334. For extensive critique of this earlier view, as well as careful reconstructions of the social level of Christians in the Corinthian churches, see Meeks, *First Urban Christians*, 53–72; Theissen, *Social Setting*, 70–96.

from the "laboring and burdened" classes. In all probability, the community was composed of people from a wide range of social strata, as in the congregations about which more is known (e.g., Rome, Corinth, or Thessalonica), and as the Roman governor Pliny would observe to be true in the province of Bithynia (*Ep.* 10.96).

SOCIAL HISTORY OF THE GROUP

If we attend to the data within the sermon "to the Hebrews," we find that the author specifically recalls three important phases of the community's history, giving us the basis for a profile of the community's formative experiences. The author strategically selects these episodes to serve his own rhetorical goals rather than to satisfy ours. Nevertheless, they provide three windows through which we may peer into the life and history of this community.

The first episode concerns the conversion of the audience, or at least the formation of the community's core, as a response to hearing those who were Jesus' witnesses proclaim the gospel in their location. The author recalls that the community experienced what it understood as supernatural confirmation of the truth of the message, as "God bore witness alongside" the preachers "with signs and wonders and various miracles, and by gifts of the Holy Spirit, distributed according to his will" (Heb 2:4). The evangelistic experience described by the author closely resembles Paul's reminiscences of his own founding of the churches in Galatia and Corinth (Gal 3:2–5; 1 Cor 2:1–5), where he also draws explicit attention to the encounter with the divine as the ultimate foundation of the community's new allegiances.

Sociologist Emile Durkheim would describe this kind of group experience as "collective effervescence," whereby the group experiences something more powerful together than can be attributed to the contributions of the sum of its members.[16] This "something more" is understood as an experience of the proximity of the divine, such that the group, its gatherings, and its foundational *ratio* are invested with the charismatic legitimation bestowed upon that which brings people into closer contact with "the ultimate." This experience was sufficient to motivate the audience to make a decisive break with their former understandings of how the divine operated and was accessed, and with the social networks sustained by (and sustaining) those understandings.

The author refers, secondly, to the elements of a process by means of which the converts were socialized into the worldview of the new group and forged into a new community (5:11—6:3). They were introduced to the Jewish Scriptures as "the oracles of God" (5:12) and initiated into a Christ-centered reading of the same together, no doubt, with traditions about Jesus' life and teachings ("the basic teaching about Christ," 6:1a). The author specifically speaks of the "foundation" of their socialization into the Christian community as involving "repentance from dead works and faith toward God, instruction about baptisms and laying on of hands, and resurrection of the dead and eternal judgment" (6:1b–2). Each of these elements is rich with Jewish and Christian cultural references. Gentiles joining the Christian community would be unfamiliar with many if not all of these

---

16. Durkheim, *Elementary Forms*, 240.

elements,[17] while Jews converted to belief in Jesus would need reorientation to these basic facets of their own worldview in terms of their relationship now to the person and work of Jesus. Having to learn "faith in God" particularly recalls the socialization of Gentiles into the Christian community (1 Thess 1:9; Acts 14:15).

The topic of "repentance from dead works" highlights the attention given in this stage to helping the converts make a decisive break with particular facets of their pre-conversion lives and practices. The "dead works" (*erga nekra*) are not the "external regulations associated with the Levitical priesthood in the earthly sanctuary,"[18] hence the audience's prior involvement in Judaism. The author never critiques the Levitical sacrifices themselves as "dead works" from which the audience had to repent, but as an ineffective means of cleansing the conscience from "dead works" of some other sort, a cleansing that Jesus at last accomplished (9:9–14; see also 10:1–4). The author might use "dead works," in the first instance, to refer to idols. Both times he uses this phrase, "dead works" are contrasted with faith toward or the worship of the "living God" (6:1; 9:14). This contrast, furthermore, is basic to the definition of "them" as opposed to "us" in both Jewish and Christian literature (e.g., Ps 96:4–5; 97:7; 1 Thess 1:9). The only verbal parallel to the expression occurs in Wis 15:17 in the context of the author's polemic against idol worship: "being mortal, they make a dead thing [*ergazetai nekron*] with lawless hands." This author frequently calls idols "dead things" (*nekra*, Wis 13:10,

17. In and of themselves, these six elements are so basic as to presuppose no knowledge even of Jewish worldview, ethos, and practice (so Attridge, *Hebrews*, 163).

18. Lane, *Hebrews 1–8*, 140; Stedman, *Hebrews*, 69.

18; 15:5). The phrase might also express "works leading to death," and, thus, behaviors contrary to the law of God (cf. Deut 30:15–20), the outcome of which is death.[19]

Whether one argues for a specific or more general referent, the social effects of this language are clear: the converts' prior life was a life of "dead works," works with no value, life, or honor. By contrast, the works they have done since their conversion, particularly their "works of mutual love and service" (6:9), are "noble works" (10:24; 13:21), works that God keeps alive in God's memory with a view to rewarding the doer. Characterizing life before a convert's association with the Christian community as "dead" strategically reinforces commitment to the new community while helping believers dissociate themselves from their own pre-Christian identity, behaviors, and associations (compare the similar techniques found in Rom 6:17–18; 1 Cor 6:9–11; Eph 5:8; Col 1:13; 1 Pet 2:9–10).

The third pair, "resurrection of the dead and eternal judgment," identifies two essential elements of the Jewish and Christian worldview. These elements elevate God's judgment of the individual person above the opinion of any human court, since God's evaluation determines one's honor or lack of honor for the eternity beyond this life. Because God's approval or disapproval is known only through the knowledge imparted within the group and its sacred tradition, grounding converts in the belief of a life beyond death, the quality of which is determined by God's judgment, is a powerful tool for maintaining commitment to the minority culture's way of life. Where Jews or Christians are firmly convinced of this view

19. Nelson, *Raising*, 146, calling attention to the "sin unto death" in 1 John 5:16.

of reality, they will frequently choose to die before choosing to defect from the group or depart from its values and practices, since perseverance leads to "eternal reward" and violation brings the threat of "eternal punishment." The author of Hebrews will rely heavily on these facets of the group's worldview throughout his sermon as a basis for his exhortations (see Heb 1:14; 2:1–3, 10; 4:12–13; 5:9; 10:26–31, 36–39; 12:26–28; 13:4).

The middle pair of topics identifies rituals that played an important role in effecting the transition from outsider to insider. The plural form "baptisms" or "washings" (*baptismoi*) is unexpected, and surely not accidental. Baptism was the primary rite of initiation into the Christian community in the Pauline mission and, from what we can tell, the practice of the Christian movement as a whole. The author's language would surely evoke memories of this boundary-making ritual among the audience. What other "washing" or "washings" the author had in mind besides this remains uncertain. It may be that he is alluding to some early teaching that contrasted baptism with pagan ablutions or Jewish purification rites,[20] or to a distinctive practice of purificatory rites alongside baptism otherwise unattested in the early church.[21] The author may also be alluding to his own understanding of the cleansing of the believer, which he will articulate more fully in 10:22. There he speaks of twin washings, one involving "clean water" for the cleansing of the body and one involving the cleansing of the heart "from a bad conscience" by Jesus' death (applying 9:11—10:18). A third possibility, given that the author speaks

20. See Spicq, *Hébreux*, 2:148; Moffatt, *Hebrews*, 75; Lane, *Hebrews 1–8*, 140.

21. Attridge, *Hebrews*, 164.

of receiving a share in the Holy Spirit quite soon after mentioning "baptisms and laying on of hands" (6:4), is that the author has in mind the double baptisms featured prominently in Acts, namely water baptism and the baptism of the Holy Spirit. As this question is, for the present time, insoluble, we will focus on the one certain element, namely, baptism as a rite of initiation into the Christian group.

The ritual of baptism, particularly where practiced as immersion of the whole person in water, can profoundly impact those being baptized, effecting a powerful change in the baptizands' perception of themselves and their relation to old and new social relationships. Victor Turner's description of the "ritual process" observed in rites of passage involving changes in a person's status within a group (for example, a person's transition from childhood to adulthood, or from common status to chieftain) provides a helpful cross-cultural perspective.[22] The initial phase of these rituals involves breaking down the status and identity that the initiate had prior to the ritual, leaving the person (or group of persons) "marginal" or "liminal" with regard to the larger society, since the person no longer fits within that society's lines of classification. As the ritual proceeds, a new status and identity is formed, sometimes in the context of forming a strong bond with other initiates (as in group rites of passage). At the end of the ritual, the person is reintegrated into society on the basis of this new status or identity (as well as with the sense of solidarity with fellow initiates, where applicable).

Baptism functions similarly as a rite of passage. Paul (and we recall that the author of Hebrews most likely addresses an audience connected somehow with the Pauline mission)

22. Turner, *Ritual Process*, 94–165.

speaks of baptism in terms of dying and coming to life again anew (Rom 6:3–12). The rite itself provides a mechanism that helps initiates to "die to their old life" and be "reborn to the new."[23] Baptism involves the washing away of past sins (Heb 10:22; see also Acts 2:38), and thus the renunciation of some elements of one's life experienced apart from and prior to joining the group and, thereby, the erection of barriers between oneself and one's former life and its social structures. It symbolically enacts his or her "death" to that former life matrix, his or her renunciation of former allegiances, affiliations, and relations.[24] Whatever status or identity they had before the rite, the baptismal waters wash it away (cf. 1 Cor 6:11). The initiates rise from the water with a wholly new identity (for example, "children of God") and emerge to join a new community, the "sanctified," who were themselves "washed with pure water" (Heb 10:22). Mircea Eliade expresses this most poetically: "In water, everything is 'dissolved,' every 'form' is broken up, everything that has happened ceases to exist; nothing that was before remains after immersion in water. . . . Breaking up all forms, doing away with the past, water possesses this power of purifying, of regenerating, of giving new birth."[25]

Turner's model, however, does not precisely fit Christian baptism in one important regard. He studies rites of passages in which the initiates are reintegrated into the same society from which they were ritually separated in a liminal or marginal state. In baptism, the initiate enters into an unending state of liminality in regard to society, even while he or she is integrated into a new society, the society of the Christian

23. Douglas, *Purity and Danger*, 96.
24. Kanter, *Commitment*, 73.
25. Eliade, *Patterns*, 194.

minority group. Their new identity and status is recognized within the sect, not by the society. In this instance, the initiates are compelled "to inhabit the fringes and interstices of the social structure . . . and to [remain] . . . in a permanent liminal state, where . . . the optimal conditions inhere for the realization of communitas."[26] This is especially significant for understanding the rhetorical strategy of Hebrews, whose author develops at great length the theme of a pilgrimage faith and the need for believers to voluntarily identify themselves as "foreigners and resident aliens" (11:13–16; see also 13:13) in regard to the cities in which the converts continue to live, embracing life in the margins "outside the camp," where Jesus has gone ahead of them and for them (13:13–14).

The second rite, the "laying on of hands," is a widely attested practice of the early church, serving multiple functions including healing, imparting the Holy Spirit, and commissioning for a particular service or office. The author does not specify which function primarily applies here though, since he is speaking of foundational elements and experiences in the audience's re-socialization, he most likely has in mind the imposition of hands after a person's baptism, confirming that rite and imparting the Holy Spirit as God's anointing (see 2:4; 6:4). Converts were thus also "endowed with additional powers to enable them to cope with their new station in life."[27] The converts' new access to God's power and their experience of the Spirit's "gifts" in their midst (2:4) served as a proof and a reminder that a significant change had taken place in the converts' lives. The immediacy of the divine presence changed the converts' experience of the world and of their social and

26. Turner, *Ritual*, 145.
27. Ibid., 95.

behavioral patterns prior to their initiation.[28] Insofar as they were aware of having "drawn near" to the divine by virtue of having drawn near to and entered the Christian group, their view of life outside that group became decidedly more negative and their commitment to remain "insiders" (and, therefore, the group's boundaries) was strengthened.

The converts were thus exposed to a comprehensive process of socialization, one that heightened the boundaries between the group and the larger society at every point. Their rejection of former values, practices, and associations, however, provoked significant counter-reactions from their non-Christian neighbors. The author recalls this counter-reaction and the group's responses to it at some length, which is itself significant given how little he otherwise reveals of their history.

> Remember the earlier days during which, after you were enlightened, you endured a hard contest with sufferings. You were publicly exposed to reproaches and afflictions; you also became partners of those being thus treated. For you showed sympathy to the imprisoned and you joyfully accepted the seizure of your property, knowing that you possessed better and lasting possessions. (10:32–34)

The author does not specify how long ago the events of the "earlier days" took place, though he does indicate elsewhere that, by the time he writes, the audience had been converts for an adequate length of time for the author to expect greater rootedness in the sect's convictions and, therefore, greater readiness to act to reinforce one another's commitment to these convictions than he was currently observing (5:11–14).

28. Neitz, *Charisma and Community*, 153.

Nevertheless, the society reacted most negatively to the formation of this new group, with its distinctive ethos, in its midst.

The author's description shows that what was chiefly at stake was the honor of those who identified themselves with the Christian community in the eyes of their neighbors. These believers became the target of society's deviancy-control techniques, most notably shaming, which aimed at coercing the believers to return to a lifestyle that demonstrated their allegiance to the society's values and commitments. Honor was a primary social value in the cultures of the first-century Mediterranean. The bestowal or recognition of a person's honor ("value") or the withholding of such recognition—even the concerted application of disgrace to the person—constituted a group's primary means of reinforcing commitment to the group's values and to the behaviors that embodied those values in group-sustaining ways (for example, public beneficence, diligence in raising a family, or appropriate displays of piety toward the gods). Seneca, a first-century Roman senator and philosopher, observed that "that which is honorable is held dear for no other reason than because it is honorable" (*Ben.* 4.16.2). "Honorable" and "disgraceful" were the foundational values upon which every other set of values was grounded and coordinated.[29]

The Christian community addressed by the author had been subjected to open reviling, being held up to ridicule and shame in a "public show" (10:33a). Their neighbors verbally challenged their value and character since the shift in their allegiance and behavior, and even added physical assaults as a

29. I have discussed this at length in regard to witnesses from classical antiquity and New Testament texts in my *Honor, Patronage, Kinship & Purity*, 23–93, and at greater length in my *Despising Shame* (rev. ed.), 1–155.

means of amplifying this challenge to their honor. The latter were not intended merely to "correct" through inflicting pain, but by inscribing shame through the treatment of the physical body (as both honor and disgrace are frequently displayed in acts pertaining to the body, for example the crowning of the head or the removal of the head to be displayed on a pike).[30]

Their neighbors were so intent on stemming the growth of this group that they managed to have some of them imprisoned, on what charges we can only speculate. The identification of a person as a "Christian" was not yet a crime, but it would be easy enough to manufacture charges against members of a potentially subversive and unpopular group. It is noteworthy that those members of the community that escaped being targeted for public disgrace voluntarily identified with "those who were thus treated," bearing witness to their fellow Christians and to the society that the bond forged within the group was stronger than fear of the society's power to shame. Prisoners in the Greco-Roman world relied on family and friends from the outside to provide for their basic needs (food beyond subsistence, clothing, medicine). The addressees of Hebrews exhibited this kind of care for their own, even at risk to themselves.[31]

The "seizure" of the property of some Christians could refer to plundering the unoccupied properties of the imprisoned or the still-occupied properties of those whose unpopularity would assure that they would never get a fair hearing before

30. Pitt-Rivers, "Honour and Social Status," 25. Philo of Alexandria concurs, speaking of the physical punishment suffered by Alexandrian Jews as "disgrace" or "insult" (*hybris*; In *Flacc.* 72, 77).

31. Wansink, *Chained in Christ*, 80: "Association with the imprisoned drew suspicion to oneself, and this often led to one's death." See Dio, *Or.* 58, 3.7; 11.5–6; Tacitus, *Ann.* 6.5.9; Philo, *Flacc.* 72.

local magistrates. The author might also choose to label as "plunder" a court's or local official's cooperation with popular shaming by the imposition of some kind of fine upon individual Christians. The loss of material wealth compounds the loss of honor and status, particularly if the person sustaining the loss was perceived to have brought the loss upon himself or herself, as would be the case for the audience.[32] Any loss of property could have put the believers in an uncomfortable economic position. Since their neighbors would also cease to do business with members of a group targeted for shaming, the Christians could well have found themselves in a lower economic status with no means of recovery as long as they remained associated with the suspect group.

The public imposition of disgrace constituted a principal strategy for the exercise of social control. The members of the larger society were attempting to "correct" what they perceived as deviant knowledge and deviant behavior in their midst, and to dissuade others from being attracted to this deviant group. Moreover, seeing the change in the converts' behavior was no doubt very threatening to the converts' neighbors and to the certainty of those beliefs and practices which those neighbors formerly shared with the converts who forsook them. Just as the converts had rejected their former associates and commitments when they joined the Christian group, so their rejected neighbors reaffirmed their *own* commitments, worldview, and values by rejecting the converts and branding them as "deviants."

Why did the converts' neighbors respond so negatively to their newfound religious commitments? This question would be answered differently depending on the ethnic background

32. Neyrey, "Loss of Wealth," 139.

of the particular neighbor. An absolute condition for a Gentile joining the Christian movement was the renunciation of every form of idolatrous cult or any act that involved the worship of a deity other than the God of Israel (see the stress laid on this abstinence in 1 Cor 10:14–22; 2 Cor 6:14–7:1; 1 Thess 1:9). Giving the gods due reverence and gratitude through the language of cult and sacrifice was deemed an essential characteristic of the virtuous citizen, who was doing his or her part to assure that the gods would continue to show favor to the community of which that citizen was a part. Withdrawal from all such demonstrations would be viewed as an affront to the gods and, therefore, a danger to the city as a whole. Demonstrating one's commitment to one's duty toward the gods, moreover, symbolized one's commitment to one's duty toward the state, authorities, friends, and family. People who failed to acknowledge the gods' claim on their lives and service could hardly be counted upon to honor the claims of state, law, family, and traditional values. The dimensions of piety and civic solidarity were connected practically as well. Acts of piety towards one or another god or goddess constituted a part of almost every political, business, and social enterprise in the Greco-Roman world.[33] Withdrawing from such settings—especially in numbers—would have been considered antisocial and even subversive.

Non-Christian Jews would have disapproved of seeing their own coreligionists joining the Christian sect for other reasons. While joining the church may have brought Gentiles closer to the God of Israel, in many instances it would have been seen to draw Jews further away, particularly in terms of

33. On the pervasiveness of religion in all aspects of life in Greco-Roman society, see MacMullen, *Paganism*, 38–39, 47.

their diligent observance of the terms of the Mosaic covenant. Their allegiance to Jesus, more widely viewed as a messianic *pretender* at best, a blasphemer and sorcerer at worst, would have reinforced the problematic nature of their conversion to that particular sect. And, of course, the nature of that sect's claims about the place of the parent religion (non-Christian Judaism) in the plan and favor of God, such as the author of Hebrews himself evidences (8:1–13!), would have been an entirely unacceptable affront.

The goal of all non-Christian Gentiles and Jews was the same in regard to the "discipline" they inflicted upon their wayward neighbors—to correct the dangerous and vicious errors of deviant fellow citizens and co-religionists by any means necessary.[34] The Christian community's response, however, was to remain firm in their commitment to the minority group and to one another, sustaining one another through mutual assistance and caring ("love and good works," 6:9–10). They persevered in their new identity and associations in the face of their neighbor's strong disapproval and attempts to exert social pressure. The community lived thus in a state of high tension with the surrounding society, a tension that clarified and reinforced the boundaries between sect and society rather than eroding the same.

PRESENTING CHALLENGES

Our only window into the situation of the addressees at the time of writing is the text of the author's response *to* that situation. We are thus wholly dependent on "mirror-reading"—

34. In 1 Thess 2:13–16, Paul provides an interesting correlation of pressures endured by Jewish and Gentile Christians from both the Roman citizens of Thessalonica and the Jewish residents of Judea.

trying to discern the challenges and circumstances of the audience from a communication addressing the audience.[35] The author makes few direct comments concerning the addressees, though he does identify one specific problem at one point: some members of the community have ceased joining in the meetings of the group. He urges the audience, "do not abandon the assembling of yourselves together," and immediately admits that this "is the habit of some" (10:25). He also upbraids them for not exhibiting the maturity in their Christian commitments that he would have expected of people who had enjoyed such rich experiences of the divine for as long as they have, expressing specific disappointment that they were waiting for him to intervene rather than taking a more active role themselves in "teaching" those who were faltering (5:12).

He describes the immediate danger facing the hearers in terms of their "drifting away" from the message (the divine word!) they heard at their conversion (2:1), their "neglecting" the message spoken by Jesus and certified by God (2:3–4), their "turning away from the living God" through distrust (3:12–13), their "failing to attain" entry into the promised place of rest (4:1), falling short in the same way as the wilderness generation on account of a failure of trust (4:12), and their "growing weary" and "losing heart" (12:3), again "falling short of [attaining] God's gift" (12:15). As the author reviews their present situation in light of their past experience, he speaks of them as having received God's gifts, but standing in some danger of failing to bear fruit through persistence and continued investment in one another (6:4–8), needing to be urged by him to remain committed to this continued investment (6:9–12;

35. For an excellent methodological introduction to reliable strategies for mirror reading, see Barclay, "Mirror-Reading."

13:1–3). Failure to do so would amount to "trampling under-foot the Son of God, regarding as common the blood by which you are sanctified, and insulting the Spirit of grace" (10:29). If there is one emphasis to which the author returns again and again, it is his encouragement that they not succumb to any faltering in commitment, but rather continue to move in the same direction in which they started heading when they first joined themselves to the Christian movement, with the same confident boldness that they formerly displayed (3:6, 14; 4:11; 6:9–12; 10:23–25, 35–36, 39; 12:1, 3, 12–13; 13:12–14).

This survey of the text suggests that the presenting problem does not have to do with what the author considers deviant theology, for example, a tendency toward angel worship. Such suggestions are examples of questionable mirror reading, insofar as they ignore explicit statements in the text and pervading the text in favor of looking at 1:4–14 (and the situation behind Colossians) as an inverted view of the problem.[36] Neither is the presenting problem the threat of looming persecution, for the author describes the hearers as in danger of "drifting away," or "not giving due attention" to the deliverance Jesus has provided, or "being sluggish in heeding" the word—not as people about to be asked to pay the ultimate price.[37] Rather, the author addresses a community some of whose members are faltering in their commitment—their assurance that the "word" they received is reliable, their conviction that they have indeed encountered the divine

36. Jewett, *Pilgrims*, 10–13.

37. The author's assertion that the audience has "not yet resisted to the point of blood" (12:4) does not suggest that their blood is about to be required. Rather, it points out to them that, however costly their commitment to Jesus has been, they have not yet begun to pay to sustain the relationship as Jesus had paid to create it.

as a result of joining this group, their certainty that the rewards promised are real and worth the price they have paid to remain associated with the group to whom the rewards were promised. They have lived too long without honor in the world and without having received the "glory" that was promised to God's "sons and daughters" (2:10).

The danger of falling away now presents itself because of the lingering effects of the believers' loss of status and esteem in their neighbors' eyes, and their inability to recover their place in society or their neighbors' approval by any means that would also allow them to remain rigidly faithful to the One God. The community experienced the loss of property and status in the host society without yet receiving the promised rewards of the sect. This place "in between"—this *liminal* place—is difficult to occupy, and so some members, at least, are growing disillusioned with the sect's promise to provide. As people sensitive to honor and shame, and as time passes without improvement of their status through God's intervention, they begin to feel the inward pressure again for the larger society's affirmation and approval. Their earlier fervor has cooled and their earlier certainty has been eroded by their prolonged exposure to their neighbors, the agents and witnesses of their degradation, who probably continued to disparage the believers as subversive and shameful.[38] Though they were able to resist their neighbors' attempts to shame them for quite some time, the machinery of social control is

---

38. Aristotle observes that people "are more likely to be ashamed when they have to be seen and to associate openly with those who are aware of their disgrace" (*Rhet.* 2.6.27). The inhabitants of the Mediterranean world were not above taunting those whom they considered "undesirables" or whom they wished to shame (see Ps 108:25 for but one complaint).

beginning, in the long run, to succeed in wearing down the deviants' resistance. While they could accept their loss in the fervor of religious solidarity, living with their loss (and continually fighting back the desire to enjoy once more the goods and esteem of their society) has proven difficult. As some individuals grew more aware of the price than the prize, they began to draw away from open association with the Christian community. To their neighbors, such withdrawal could only be seen as a good thing, a step toward "recovery" that they would have been quick to affirm. The author does not know how widespread or deep this faltering in commitment runs, but he sees the warning signs not only in the furtive defection of the few but also in the lack of vigor in community interaction and mutual reinforcement that would allow such defection even to become a possibility.

The occasion for Hebrews, then, has a distinctly sociological dimension. The host society has exerted, over time, significant social pressure upon a sectarian group in its midst with a view to curtailing its growth and "rehabilitating" its members. The sect, in turn, has experienced the challenges of maintaining commitment to that group and to the beliefs and practices that gave rise to the "mutual antagonism" between sect and society. Maintaining this "sectarian tension" with the host society has taken an obvious toll in terms of the material and social resources of the group's members. The ongoing experience of social pressure from outside threatens to lead either to the defection from the sect of members as they do *not*, in fact, "see the Day drawing closer" (10:25) or to the lessening of tension as the sectarian group accommodates its identity, message, and practices to the society around it.

In the case of the group addressed by Hebrews, the former danger is the greater one.[39]

The author's agenda and strategy is similarly sociological (or, at least, readily amenable to sociological analysis). His goal is to motivate the hearers to persevere in their commitment to one another, to the sacred *ratio* at the core of the sect's formation, and to the ethos (the values and practices) that the sect's *ratio* nurtures. In other words, he wants to see the community maintain the identity, practices, and boundaries that led to its experience of high tension with the society, and thus to persist in maintaining that very tension (rather than defect or compromise).

Everything in his sermon from beginning to end can be understood as a rhetorical incentive or constraint aimed at achieving this goal. A number of strategies are particularly important and prominent. The author reinforces the worldview (the cosmology, the eschatology, the ultimacy of God's judgment) that allows an interpretation of these social tensions that will motivate and facilitate the ongoing endurance of the tension. He seeks to strengthen the "plausibility structure" for this world view—that is, he seeks to strengthen the social bonds and interactions of the members of the group (see, for example, 6:9–10; 10:23–25; 13:1–3), who together provide the life matrix and social support that enables the individual member to continue to hold to the sect's *ratio* as "plausible" and therefore a reliable basis for decision and action.[40] If the Christian proclamation was to be maintained,

39. In the Christian communities addressed by John's Revelation, by contrast, there appears to be greater readiness to explore the latter strategy for relieving sectarian tension, especially in the communities that show openness to "Jezebel" and "the Nicolaitans."

40. On the concept of the "plausibility structure," see ch. 5 below.

and if individual followers had any hope of continuing forward in the new direction their lives took when they joined the sect, the group within which the Christian counter-definitions of reality were validated had to be preserved. Perhaps most vitally, he seeks to insulate the group members from the society's attempts to shame them, and to reorient them to these experiences of being shamed in ways that will nullify their effects, and to shift their focus to considering the appropriateness of their own response to God and God's Son, in whose hands lies the power to ascribe eternal honor or eternal disgrace.

In the chapters that follow, we will explore three dimensions of the author's socio-rhetorical strategy for promoting his own social-formation goals for the community in relation to the non-Christian society. The first will focus on the author's strategy for reorienting the audience to the social pressure of shame, so as to defuse its power to erode commitment to the sect. The second will focus on the author's use of a fundamental set of social codes and expectations—the codes and expectations inscribed in the pervasive social institution of patronage and value of reciprocity—to foreground response to God and God's gifts and promises in the audience's weighing of costs and benefits in their setting. The third will focus on the author's promotion of a particular ideology of group identity that promotes continued adherence and on the sociological strategies he puts in place to promote strong, centripetally-driving group interaction.

EXCURSUS: THE DATE OF HEBREWS

There are admittedly few data within the text of Hebrews that help determine the date of composition. The likelihood that Clement of Rome depends upon and uses Hebrews as he composes his letter to the Christians in Corinth sets 96 CE as the upper limit for Hebrews.[41] The mention of Timothy, who is still considered fit for travel (13:23), also necessitates a date before the end of the first century. On the other side, the likelihood that the congregation was formed during the heyday of the Pauline mission and has already been in existence for a number of years before the author writes to them suggests an earliest possible date of composition in the mid-50s CE. I personally find the author's statements about the Levitical cult to favor a date of composition before 70 CE. Granted, the author's discussion focuses on the archaic cult of the tabernacle rather than the temple in Jerusalem. This is to be expected for a Diaspora Jew who has readier access to Exodus and Leviticus than to the actual precincts of the temple in Jerusalem. At a climactic point in his argument, he speaks about the sacrifices that "they offer perpetually" (10:1) and asks the rhetorical question: if these sacrifices ever successfully achieved the cleansing of the worshipers, "would they [the sacrifices] not have ceased to be offered?" (10:2). After 70 CE, however, these sacrifices *did* in fact cease to be offered (although for a different reason than the decisive removal of sins by means of the same). In the following verse he writes that "in these [sacrifices] there is an annual reminder of sins" (10:3), retaining the use of the present tense. When he returns to contrast Jesus with the Levitical priests, he writes that "every priest stands daily, continuing to worship and to offer over and over the same sacrifices which are never able to take away sins" (10:11). These statements are far more natural in

41. Ellingworth, "Hebrews and 1 Clement"; Hagner, *Use of the Old*, 179–95; against Theissen, *Untersuchungen*, 34–41.

a pre-70 setting, speaking as they do unanimously as though the Levitical cult is still in continuous operation and giving no indication that they are now merely a memory or matter of historical interest.[42]

While neither the case for nor the case against a pre-70 date is decisive, Hebrews reads more naturally in a pre-70 CE setting.[43]

42. Scholars in favor of a pre-70 date also point to the lack of a mention of the destruction of the temple, which might have played very well into the author's hands (Ellingworth, *Hebrews*, 32; Witherington, "Influence," 151), as it certainly did in the hands of the author of *Epistle of Barnabas*. While arguments from silence (what the text does *not* say) are always tenuous, I would disagree with those who claim that the author refused to speak of the temple's destruction out of sensitivity for his (Jewish) hearers. His unsparing critique of the inefficacy of the Levitical cultus and his affirmation of the obsolescence of Torah do not betray any hint of such sensitivity, and it is hard to see how he could have made his sermon any more offensive by speaking also of the destruction of the "copy" and "shadow."

Objections to a date prior to 70 CE are often urged on the grounds that the audience of Hebrews is dependent on the generation of witnesses to Jesus for its faith (2:3), and so represent a second generation of the church (see, e.g., Aitken, "Portraying," 133–34). Those who gathered in Jerusalem for Pentecost in 30 CE, however, were already "dependent upon others who 'heard the Lord,'" as were most if not all members of any churches founded outside of Judea and Galilee in the decade following the resurrection. Similarly, any attempt to see reflections of martyrdom (e.g., the Neronian persecution) in Hebrews are highly suspect, as the author himself points away from the hearers' firsthand exposure to bloodshed for the sake of the name (12:4).

43. For more thorough reviews of this insoluble question, see Spicq, *Hébreux*, 253–61; Attridge, *Hebrews*, 6–9.

THREE

Sociorhetorical Strategy I: Negating the Social Pressure of Shame

The social-scientific study of the Hellenistic-Roman world has demonstrated the importance of honoring and shaming as fundamental social processes by means of which a group upholds the values and practices that are central to that group's identity and persistence, and by means of which a group reinforces, through positive and negative social pressure, the commitment of its individual members to those values and practices. A significant challenge posed to any group in the period of imperialistic expansion beginning with Babylon's invasions of the West, but particularly exacerbated by Alexander, his successors, and finally Rome, is the availability of other groups promoting alternative values and practices as honorable and shameful among their adherents, and creating thus a public witness to these alternative values, challenging the givenness or taken-for-grantedness of any one group's delineations of the values and practices that are "truly" honorable or disgraceful. It was this imperialist expansion that created a Greek or Graecised elite at the upper political and economic echelons across large regions otherwise defined by non-Greek indigenous populations and indigenous cultures. It was this imperialist expansion that led, either through forced relocation or fresh opportunities, to the migration of Jews throughout the Levant and the Eastern Mediterranean, often forming clearly identifiable and close-knit communities in the midst of the dominant culture's population.

Each group developed strategies for insulating itself against the witness of other groups to alternative world constructions (including belief systems) and the alternative ethos that each world construction nurtured. The ultimate "Greek" defense, for example, was the ideology that all non-Greek cultures were "barbaric"—not just "strange" or "foreign," but "non-Greek" and therefore inferior, savage, in need of the civilizing influence of the newly dominant Greek culture. This ideology shielded many Greeks from considering as a vital option the way of life prized by an indigenous culture. While cultural blending was a vibrant reality in the centuries after Alexander, this ideology (and the ultimate power behind it) also assured that those who spoke Greek and haled from Greece remained more or less in the driver's seat of the blending process. Where an indigenous people honored something held in disrepute among Greeks, or where an indigenous population ridiculed some aspect of Greek culture, the Greek could simply say, "What should we expect from barbarians?" What was honored or censured in the subordinate group did not, therefore, need to exercise pressure upon the values and commitments of the dominant group.

Subordinate groups had to work considerably harder to insulate themselves where their core values and practices, honored and prized within their group, would be censured as shameful in another group, especially a more powerful group. The Jewish people, particularly throughout but not limited to the Diaspora, found themselves in this position in the Hellenistic and Roman periods. Jewish groups tended to hold strict observance of the covenant stipulations of Torah as a mark of honor and value. To Greeks and Romans, however, the denial of every god but one's own, the refusal to eat certain foods that were staples of the Greek or Roman diet (e.g., pork and shellfish), the refusal to work or fight on certain days (i.e., the Sabbath), and the tendency to remain in close-knit and inner-focused communities all seemed to violate the values of piety toward all the gods and of solidarity with one's fellow citizens. Jewish practices—and those who continued to perform them—were frequently the subject of ridicule, and Jews themselves found themselves the target for sporadic violence and abuse.

In such a situation, it was essential for the members of the minority culture to decide whose opinion, whose approval, ultimately mattered. The Jew who looked only to devout Jews for affirmation of her self-worth would continue to embody the values of devout Jews to attain that affirmation. Where a Jew, however, sought affirmation and acceptance from members of the Greek or Roman dominant culture, he would be pulled toward embodying the values of the Greek or Roman elite. Where those values and practices conflicted with the values and practices of his Jewish upbringing, a Jew could be drawn toward abandoning the latter. For Jewish culture to survive, then, it became essential for its promoters to exclude unsympathetic Gentiles from the Jew's "court of reputation" or "court of opinion"—that circle of significant others whose approval or disapproval mattered. The devout Jew (i.e., the Jew who would continue to remain steadfast in aligning his or her life with the practices consistent with Jewish cultural and social values) looked to God and those who were similarly committed to observe Torah for approval, and developed strategies for insulating himself or herself against the opinion—the social pressures of honoring and shaming—of non-Jews and non-committed Jews.

Similar strategies were developed by members of other minority cultures, such as those who adhered to particular philosophical schools and to voluntary associations like the early Christian community. Each minority culture gave attention to defining the circle of others that constituted the "court of reputation" whose grants of honor and shame would exercise effective social constraints upon the individual.[1] As a corollary, this involved developing strategies for setting aside the negative opinion of non-group members and insulating oneself from the social pressure they could apply. All groups are using the application of honor and disgrace to enforce the values of their particular culture, so each must insulate its members from the "pull" of the opinion of those outside that group.[2]

1. One finds this frequently in philosophical texts, wherein the opinion of the many is contrasted unfavorably with the value of the approval of the few or the one who has devoted his or her life to wisdom and virtue (cf. Plato, *Cri.* 44C; 46C–47A; Seneca, *Constant.* 11.2; 13.2, 5; 16.3; Epictetus, *Diss.* 1.29.50–54; 4.5.22; Dio, *Or.* 77/78.21, 25).

2. See deSilva, *Despising Shame*, 86–155, for a discussion of how several Greco-Roman philosophers and Jewish authors met this challenge; and idem, *Hope of Glory*, for a study of the challenges of maintaining Christian community in the face of the social pressures of honor and shame (and the internal use of the same to nurture adherence to group

The presenting problem that occasioned Hebrews appears to be that some members of the Christian community have begun to feel the weight of society's shaming techniques, the insults and abuse calculated to bring them, as deviants, back in line with the more dominant culture's or cultures' values and worldview. They were able to resist these pressures in the past, but continued exposure to censure and to socioeconomic marginalization has begun to erode commitment sufficiently that an unspecified number have even stopped gathering with the Christian community (10:25). If the members of the Christian minority culture are to remain committed to their alternative values and practices, they need to have their self-respect grounded again in the group's values and definitions of what makes a person "honorable," and to be insulated from the shaming strategies of non-Christians.

The author of Hebrews meets this challenge in part by holding up as praiseworthy models for imitation precisely those people who chose a lower status in this world for the sake of attaining greater and more lasting honor and advantages. The so-called encomium on faith (11:1—12:3) occupies considerable space in this oration. In this encomium, the author honors figures from the distant and recent past (in the sacred history of the group) who have exhibited the virtue of trust and loyalty toward God, and who have obtained an honorable remembrance before God and in the memory of the group specifically by despising the evaluation others made of them, embracing a less honorable status in the opinion of the dominant culture, and persevering courageously in enduring that temporarily lower status and its hardships.

---

values and commitment) in Matthew, John, 1 and 2 Corinthians, 1 and 2 Thessalonians, and Revelation.

HONORABLE EXAMPLES OF DESPISING SHAME

One social function of an encomium—a public address praising a civic benefactor, a group of fallen soldiers, or a revered
figure from the past or present—was to strengthen an audience's commitment to the values the figure or figures embodied.
Hearing others praised aroused emulation of the behaviors
that led to such esteem in the hopes of augmenting one's
own honor in the group's estimation. Even in a deliberative
speech—one aimed at persuading an audience to take or avoid
a particular course of action—a speaker often incorporated
shorter sections of encomium, celebrating the honor that others achieved in the past by embracing a course of action similar
to the course that the speaker was promoting now.

The author of the Letter to the Hebrews makes good use
of this strategy. He is fundamentally concerned with renewing the audience's commitment to persevere in association
with the Christian community and in the practice of its distinctive way of life. He does this in an essentially deliberative
environment, since two courses of action lay fairly evidently
before the audience (the other course having been visually
demonstrated in the withdrawal of some of their members).
At one point the author identifies the essential virtue that is
required to continue forward in commitment to the group as
"faith" or "faithfulness" (*pistis*). The way for the audience to
attain God's promised inheritance is by trusting and remaining loyal to their patron and benefactor, God:

> You have need of endurance in order that, having
> done the will of God, you may receive the promise.
> . . . For yet "but a little while" and "the one who is
> coming will come and not delay: and my righteous

one will live by faith [*pistis*], and if he or she shrinks back, my soul has no pleasure in that one." But we are not characterized by shrinking back unto destruction but by faith [*pistis*] unto the attainment of life. (10:36–39)

The author also names the opposite course of action here, calling it "shrinking back" (*hypostolē*) from where "trust" and "faithfulness" lead. The author strengthens his exhortation to continue in "trust" by including an encomium that celebrates the honor and approval that the revered figures of the community's sacred tradition attained in God's eyes by acting in "trust" themselves, hoping thereby to stir up the audience's waning zeal for honor before God and to reinforce the detachment of Christians from society's honor rating.

Where the author pauses to develop a particular example within this encomium, this example consistently features an element of setting aside the larger society's definitions of what is honorable and disgraceful in order to respond obediently to the call of God, where that call involved embracing a course of action or a status that outsiders would label "disgraceful" as the means to attaining greater and lasting honor before God. The examples of Abraham, Moses, the martyrs, and Jesus—and the model of the community's own past that precedes and introduces this encomium (10:32–36)—all share this common feature. Renouncing the honor and approval that accompany success and integration into the unbelieving society, they have all borne witness to a hope for something greater—the eternal benefaction promised by God—and, in their loyal obedience to this hope have accepted marginality with regard to human networks of honor and status.

Jesus, the Perfecter of "Faith"

The climactic example of the virtue of "faith/faithfulness" in action is Jesus himself. Jesus was faith's "pioneer," on whom the addressees must fix their gaze as they follow their forerunner (see 6:19–20). Jesus was also faith's "perfecter," embodying the virtue in the extreme and showing how faith achieves its goal.[3] Hebrews 12:1–3 is thus the capstone of the author's encomium, and not to be read separately from it. The exemplars of faith in chapter 11 are the people who fill the stands of spectators in 12:1, who now watch the audience run the same race, having the benefit of Jesus' crowning example.

Jesus showed "faith/faithfulness" in its fullest expression when "he endured a cross, despising shame," and this same faith led to the honor that followed, when "he sat down at the right hand of God" (12:2). The phrase "despising shame" neatly encapsulates the author's goal of detaching his audience from valuing the larger society's approval or disapproval, since it is concern for reputation in the eyes of non–group members that pulls believers away from the group and its values, leading them to assimilate back into the dominant culture. The audience of Hebrews, having accepted the loss of honor and status in order to remain loyal to God and Christ in the "earlier days," would certainly be sensitive to the loss of honor and status that Jesus endured on their behalf in order to secure the promised benefits of children of God for them.

3. Many translations render Heb 12:2 as "Jesus, the pioneer and perfecter of *our* faith" (e.g., KJV, RSV, NRSV, NIV, ESV, NLT), but there is no support in the Greek for limiting "faith" as "our faith" (so, correctly, NASV, CEB). Rather, the author names Jesus as the one who most perfectly embodies the virtue of "faith," and who therefore serves as its best exemplar.

Jesus' move into places of lower status began with the incarnation, when God "made him lower than the angels for a little while" before "crowning him with glory and honor" (Heb 2:5–7, interpreting Ps 8:4–6; cp. Phil 2:6–11). Christ's humiliation climaxes, as in the Philippians hymn, in the crucifixion. The author speaks of Jesus' suffering at several points in his sermon (2:10, 18; 5:8), but only gives it the specific shape of a cross in 12:2, a death which occurs "outside the camp" (13:11), in a place of dishonor and uncleanness. Closely connected with this death is the "hostility" (*antilogia*, 12:4) that Jesus endured, recalling the insults and ridicule that Jesus had to endure during his trial and crucifixion.[4] This aspect of the passion resonates deeply with the addressees' own experience of "reproaches and sufferings" (10:32–34).

Death on a cross was, by both Jewish and Greco-Roman standards, an utterly degrading end, not to be mentioned in polite company. Crosses with the writhing or rotting bodies fixed to them were revolting sights, rendering unclean the space they occupied. Crucifixion was associated with "the lower classes, i.e., slaves, violent criminals and the unruly elements in rebellious provinces."[5] It was painfully public, the victim being nailed up as a public example of the behaviors most especially to be avoided rather than imitated. "By the public display of a naked victim at a prominent place . . . crucifixion also represented his uttermost humiliation."[6] It was a

4. So John Chrysostom, *Hom. Heb.* (NPNF1 14:494; Migne, PG 63.196): "The blows upon the cheek, the laughter, the insults, the reproaches, the mockeries, all these he indicated by 'contradiction' (*antilogia*)."

5. Hengel, *Crucifixion*, 87. Hengel supplies a wealth of primary materials documenting the nature of, and reactions to, crucifixion in antiquity.

6. Ibid. Philo (In *Flacc.* 74, 85) also described the crucifixion of the Alexandrian Jewish senators as a "spectacle and show."

gruesome, shameful death that left nothing of the crucified's honor intact, with no possibility of redress. In the public eye, Jesus' crucifixion destroyed his honor and memory. For the author of Hebrews, however, this same death exemplifies the perfection of the virtue of faith and the pattern that leads to the rewards of faith. Paradoxically, the path to honor before God entailed the "despising of the shame" that human society could inflict.

The phrase "despising shame" does not merely indicate that Jesus "braved" the experience of humiliation that the cross entailed,[7] but that he counted it no "shame" at all on account of enduring it for the sake of obedience to God and of bringing benefit to many. If those who ridiculed and derided him failed to recognize this, their ignorance brought no true shame upon him. In Plutarch's *Life of Cato the Younger*, the devotee of philosophy is said to train himself or herself to "be ashamed only of what was truly shameful, and otherwise to despise what people called shameful" (6.6). Cato displays independence from the society's definitions of honor and shame and its use of sanctions to enforce these definitions, preferring to take his bearings from his philosophy rather than succumbing to social pressures to adopt or abstain from certain behaviors.

When Jesus, similarly, "despises shame," he sets aside sensitivity to others' evaluation of his actions and commitments for the sake of persevering in the course of action to which God has called him, so as to have God's approval. When one "despises shame," then, one sets aside concern for one's reputation in the eyes of the unenlightened, and simultaneously places a negative value on the opinion of those who would judge one's actions as disgraceful. This corresponds to

7. So Delitzsch, *Hebrews*, 306; Lane, *Hebrews 9–13*, 414.

the philosopher's setting aside of the evaluation non-philosophers formed of his or her values, goals, and behavior. The person unacquainted with the truth was like a child, whose opinion counted for nothing.[8] Those who were dedicated to different ideals belonged in two different courts of reputation that did not intersect. By using this phrase, the author claims that Jesus was aware that the society that held him in contempt was unaware of what was truly valuable and honorable in God's sight, and therefore their evaluation of him simply did not affect his true honor in the least—a conviction confirmed by his subsequent exaltation to God's right hand.

This was precisely the way in which the early church fathers read Heb 12:2: Jesus, as "lord of glory" was in a position to despise the opinion unenlightened human beings held of him (Origen, *Fr. Ps.* 37.12.4–5; Gregory of Nyssa, *Eunom.* 3.5). Moreover, these early interpreters understand the importance of this facet of Jesus' model for the believers.[9] In his *Exhortatio ad Martyrium* (37.11–14), written in the period of the Decian persecution, Origen encourages the Christians to resist both social and physical pressures placed on them by holding up Jesus, as presented in Heb 12:2, as an example: "Thus Jesus endured a cross, despising shame, and because of this was seated at God's right hand. Those who imitate him, despising shame, will also be seated with him and rule with him in the heavens." John Chrysostom, commenting on this verse, also interprets Jesus' example as modeling the rejection of the opinion of unbelievers for Chrysostom's hearers.

8. See Aristotle, *Rhet.* 2.6.14–15; Seneca, *Constant.* 13.2.

9. This is also noted by modern commentators (see Weiß, *Hebräer,* 639; Attridge, *Hebrews,* 357–58).

By accepting a shameful death Jesus taught his followers "to count as nothing the opinion of human beings."[10]

Aristotle spoke of the praise accruing to the one who submits "to some disgrace or pain for the sake of attaining [*anti*] some great and noble object" (*Eth. nic.* 3.1.7), claiming that a noble goal and result can redeem the one who has suffered some disgrace as praiseworthy and honorable. The author of Hebrews, seeking to hold up as a model of exemplary behavior one who suffered the greatest disgrace, thus names the lofty goal on the basis of which Jesus' honor is reestablished. Jesus could disregard society's impositions of (extreme) shaming and persevere in obedience to God because he looked to the reward accompanying such obedience: he endured the cross "for the sake of the joy that was set before him,"[11] namely being "seated at God's right hand" (12:2). The larger society did not have all the facts, as it were, and so its judgments and evaluations were unreliable and unsound. The end result of honor before God vindicates the one who chooses obedience to God even if it entails disgrace before society. The unbelieving society might continue to regard Jesus as a disgraced criminal, but before the court of God Jesus holds the highest honor: his taking his seat at God's right hand proves that he remained above reproach, and that he had in fact acted honorably. Hebrews thus encourages the readers to take their bearings also from the perspective of the heavenly reward, from which vantage point their experiences of dishonor are transformed into a noble contest for an honorable prize.

10. John Chrysotom, *Hom. Heb.* (NPNF1 14:493; Migne, PG 63.194).

11. On interpreting the preposition *anti* here as "for the sake of" rather than "instead of," see deSilva, *Perseverance*, 435–38.

Jesus, the example of faith *par excellence*, enacts his faith by choosing the course of action that fulfills the value of obedience to God without regard for the approval or disapproval of society: this is the meaning of "despising shame." Faith looks only to God's approval and seeks honor only as recognized by God's court (see ch. 5 below). Faith therefore remains steadfast in the face of the larger society or any more powerful group's attempts to pressure the Christian into conforming to its values. Jesus' exaltation, moreover, proves the rule by exemplifying the extreme: the most revolting and degrading death in the eyes of the dominant culture's representatives leads to the most exalted status in God's eyes (and in the estimation of the Christian sect).[12] The path of faith remains the way of honor, no matter what opinion society has of, or what dishonor society shows toward, the believers. God will vindicate the faithful before the eyes of the unbelieving world, when God shall "put all things under [Christ's] feet" (2:8; cf. 1:13; 10:13). On that day, God shall rule the court of human opinion out of order and overturn its former verdicts.

The Witnesses of Faith

Jesus' example is the culmination of a series of examples of faith: the famous litany of examples of faith praised in Heb 11. While the author's principles of selection are too complex to be reduced to a single one motive or intent, one thread linking those examples that the author pauses to craft and develop (Abraham and Moses), as well as the miscellany of the

12. Pitt-Rivers rightly observes that, in a complex society, "the individual's worth is not the same in the view of one group as in that of another" ("Honour and Social Status," 22).

martyrs and marginalized, is that these figures embraced a lower status in the world's eyes for the sake of the heavenly reward. That is, like Jesus, they too each "despised shame" in his or her own way. Together with Jesus, moreover, these are the examples of those who "through faith [*pistis*] and patience inherit the promises," whom the addressees are specifically called to emulate (6:11–12).

In the opening verses of this encomium, the author establishes three important points related to the virtue of "faith" that he commends to his audience. First, "faith" (*pistis*), and its opposite, "distrust" (*apistia*), are both defined in terms of a patron-client relationship between God and human beings in Hebrews (see ch. 4 below). Faith looks to God as Benefactor: the author writes that "without faith it is impossible to please God, for whoever would approach him must exercise trust that he exists and that he rewards those who seek him" (11:6; see also 10:35; 11:26). Faith trusts God for the reward of obedience and remains faithful to God in the face of any temporal social pressures with a view to enjoying this reward.

Second, faith navigates its course by the unseen and future realities, rather than taking its bearings merely from the visible and present world. The exemplars of faith are enabled to make the right choices because of this wider vision (11:3, 7, 10, 16, 20, 22, 26b, 27b, 35b). This expanded scope relativizes the value of this present, mutable world, and neutralizes the opinion of those who make value judgments based on the partial vision of looking to this world. Access to this larger picture alone enables the person of faith to endure the loss of status and prestige that the actions of faith bring in the eyes of unbelievers, and so attain life and honor before God and in the memory of the community of believers.

Third, faith leads to "attestation," a "positive witness" to the value of one's life (*martyria*, 11:2, 4, 5), gaining for the faithful a lasting testimony to their honor and worth. This term is used in civic settings to speak of the endorsement given by Roman authorities to a person whom a local assembly wished to honor.[13] The author creates an *inclusio* (a literary frame) around the whole of chapter 11 by using forms of the verb form (*martyreisthai*) in the opening verses of the litany of faith (11:3) and again at the transition from encomium to hortatory conclusion (11:39), underscoring the attestation, the "positive witness," that the highest Authority will bear in regard to the worth of Christ's faithful clients. Thus, orienting oneself toward God and walking in the path that takes into account realities and promises not yet experienced as visible, being undeterred by the negative opinion of those who stand outside the patron-client relationship with the One God and who do not perceive the larger picture of the cosmos, become the path to lasting honor.

The first figure over whom the author lingers at any length is Abraham, highlighting decidedly different aspects of Abraham's story than does Paul, for example, in Galatians or Romans:

> By faith [*pistis*] Abraham, when he was called to go out to a place that he was about to receive as an inheritance, obeyed, not knowing where he was going. By faith he lived as an alien in the land promised to him, dwelling in tents with Isaac and Jacob, the co-heirs of the same promise, for he was waiting for the city that had foundations, whose builder and architect was God. By faith Sarah, being herself

13. Danker, *Benefactor*, 442–43.

sterile, received the power to conceive offspring—
and this when she was well on in age—because she
considered the one who promised to be trustworthy [*pistos*]. Therefore from one person were born
descendants like the stars in heaven in number and
like the innumerable sands by the shore of sea—and
these from someone who had been as good as dead.

These all died aligned with trust [*pistis*]. They
didn't receive the promises, but saw and greeted
them from a distance, confessing themselves to
be strangers and resident aliens upon the land.
For those who speak such things make it clear
that they are seeking a homeland. And if they had
been remembering that land from which they had
gone out, they would have had the opportunity to
return. But now they are seeking a better homeland, that is, a heavenly one. Therefore God isn't
ashamed to be called *their* God, for he prepared a
city for them. (11:8–16)

Whereas Paul saw Abraham's faith exemplified in his firm
conviction that God would fulfill the promise to give him
offspring (cf. Gal 3:15–18; Rom 4:13–21), here the emphasis
falls on Abraham's voluntary departure from his native land
in obedience to God's summons (11:8–10).

In the Greco-Roman world, a person's native land gave
him or her a sense of identity and belonging. The fellow inhabitants of one's native country or city formed one's primary reference group. Dio Chrysostom, writing in the late first or early
second century, speaks of being held in honor in one's native
land as the highest good (*Or.* 44.1). Living away from one's
native land meant the loss of the status that a person enjoyed
in that native land, particularly the status that came from the
honor developed by the family over generations. This loss was

aggravated by limited access to acquiring honor in the foreign land. Indeed, sojourning as an alien was in and of itself a state of potential humiliation (Lucian, *My Native Land* 8), and the terms "exile," "foreigner," and "immigrant" could be tossed out as insults (Plutarch, *Exil.* 17 [*Mor.* 607 A]). The stranger or foreigner generally lacks citizenship in the new locale, and thus lacks the rights and protection citizenship afforded against insult, abuse, and assaults on property or honor.[14]

The audience would have heard Abraham's conscious choice, shared by his family, to embrace the life of "foreigners and resident aliens" (11:13) as a choice in favor of a lower status liable to dishonor and danger, made for the sake of obedience to God's call. This aspect of Abraham's faith reverberates most loudly with the audience's own condition (cf. 10:32–34). They had not physically moved from their native land, but they have certainly suffered social dislocation as a result of their experience of abuse and insult at the hands of their neighbors. Like Abraham outside Haran, they had left behind their former status and the dignity and security that status afforded them. The author further (and specifically) praises the patriarchs for choosing not to return to their native land and to the safety and security they once enjoyed there, pressing on instead in their quest for a "better homeland, that is, a heavenly one" (11:16). This again mirrors the addressees' situation, who must choose between renouncing Christ (and thus regaining a home in the larger society) and remaining exiles in their society for the sake of enrollment in the "city that is yet to come" (13:14). The patriarchs' faithfulness to the heavenly realm as their true native land wins them God's approval and the honor of being associated with God's name.

14. Cf. Dio, *Or.* 66.15; Philo, *Flacc.* 53–55.

By leaving their native land in obedience to God, Abraham and his family embraced the lower status of foreigners, sojourners, and strangers and the exposure to reproach and dishonor that accompanied this change of status. Nevertheless, they accepted and persevered in this status (11:13, 16), despite having the option to return to their former status in their native land (11:15). They set aside their sense of shame before the worldly court of opinion, and so were not moved to return from their marginal relationship with society to a place of honor in society's eyes. Rather, they seek only the honor of a better citizenship before God and God's approval, which they receive in the form of association with God's name (11:16).

The next well-developed example of faith in Hebrews 11 is Moses. The author again casts his description of Moses' faith to answer the situation of his congregation:

> By faith Moses refused to be called the son of Pharaoh's daughter when he had grown up, choosing to be ill-treated along with God's people rather than to enjoy the short-lived pleasure of sin. He considered the reproach that fell upon God's anointed to be worth more than the treasures of Egypt, for he was looking ahead to the reward. By faith he left Egypt behind, not fearing the king's anger, for he endured as one who saw the unseen. (11:24–27)

The author says nothing about the giving of the Law or even the great acts of the exodus. Rather, he focuses upon Moses' renunciation of status and honor in the eyes of the dominant culture and his acceptance of the degraded status of a slave in order to bind himself to the people of God and share in their future enjoyment of God's promised reward. This pattern again matches the community's own past choices (10:33–34) and what the author calls the audience to continue to choose in their present (13:3).

Moses enacts faith as he refuses "to be called a son of a daughter of Pharaoh" (11:24), recognizing that God is to be found among the oppressed Hebrews rather than the privileged elite of Egypt. In near-contemporary versions of the story, Moses refuses the throne of Egypt itself (see Philo, *Mos.* 1.13; Josephus, *Ant.* 2.9.7 §233) and the "treasures of Egypt" that would have been placed at Moses' disposal to gain honor for himself as king and benefactor. By faith, Moses renounces such status and promise of honor, disdaining the honor offered by human courts of reputation, and chooses instead to attach himself to the Hebrew slaves, people of no honor in society's eyes and subject to insult and physical outrage.

The pleasure Moses refused, however, is qualified in two important ways. First, it is merely "temporary," which stands in stark contrast to the inheritance of the faithful, frequently described as "enduring" (10:34; 12:27; 13:14). The honor and security this temporary enjoyment of worldly status and wealth bestows has no lasting value. Second, when God judges the world this temporary pleasure will yield lasting pain and disgrace, because this "pleasure" is in fact "sin" (*hamartia*, 11:25). The context here helps define "sin" in Hebrews more clearly. It is not simply a transgression of one of God's commands, but rather more specifically the rejection of living in solidarity with the people of God.[15] It means holding aloof from fellowship with God's people for the sake of the favor

15. This was observed by Theophylactus, who comments: "See, then, how he calls it sin not to endure the like injuries together with one's brothers and sisters" (Migne, PG 125:356).

and affirmation of the society that persists in ignorance and opposition to God. It is the "shrinking back" against which the author warns (10:38–39).

Moses is able to choose the loss of status and safety in the world because he properly evaluates the "reproach of the Christ" ultimately to be of greater value than "Egypt's treasures" when God's as-yet-unseen reward is thrown into the balance (11:26). The author seems to collapse time horizons when he speaks of Moses bearing "the reproach of Christ" or "the reproach of the Anointed." The phrase has its roots in pre-Christian Judaism, specifically Psalm 88:51–52, wherein the psalmist speaks of "bearing the insults of the peoples with which [God's] enemies . . . taunted the footsteps of [God's] anointed," referring to the stricken Davidic monarchy. It also connects Moses' example more closely and immediately with the audience's experience of disgrace endured because of their loyalty to Christ. The "reproach of Christ" is the lot of those who join themselves to God's people (as also Moses found) and, thus, associate themselves with the name of "Christ" (Heb 10:32; cf. 1 Pet 4:14–16; Matt 5:11; Luke 6:22). The phrase further connects Moses' example with 13:12–13, where the author exhorts the addressees to choose to bear Christ's reproach: "Therefore Jesus also suffered outside the gate in order to sanctify the people through his own blood. Therefore let us go out to him, outside the camp, bearing his reproach." The most immediate effect of this phrase would be to help the audience make the connection between Moses' praiseworthy example and the challenges of their own situation.

Moses, like Christ and Abraham, then, also "despises shame." He renounced the worldly honors that were his by birth (or adoption) and assumed the lot of a slave, choosing to join himself to God's people and their destiny, even though it entailed dishonor in the world. Moses thus provides another paradigm of faith-in-action that well suits the hearers' challenges, urging them also to continue to embrace the loss of their own place in society, to choose to remain in solidarity with the people of God through their assembling for worship (10:25) and their service to their marginalized brothers and sisters (13:3), and to persist in their pilgrimage toward the homeland of God's promise.

As he concludes his celebration of the praiseworthy heroes of faith from the pre-Christian era, the author moves from a summary of those who performed mighty and miraculous works by faith (11:32–35a) to an account of those who were tortured, killed, or otherwise disenfranchised for their commitment to God and perseverance in fulfilling the requirements of faithful clients:

> Others were tortured, refusing to accept release in order that they might attain a better resurrection. Yet others suffered the trials of ridicule, flogging, even chains and imprisonment. They were stoned to death, sawn in two, died by the edge of the sword; they wandered about clothed in the hides of sheep and goats, suffering want, oppressed, abused (the world wasn't worthy of them!), wandering about in wastelands, over mountains, and in caves and other holes in the ground. (11:35b–38)

By joining these figures to the summary of kings, warriors, and charismatic prophets, the author shows that what matters ultimately is commitment to God, not the honor or dishonor of the circumstances in which that commitment is expressed. Those who were "tortured to death" are, in God's sight, no less victorious and praiseworthy than those who "through faith conquered kingdoms."

The author refers here first to those who were tortured to death under Antiochus IV, refusing to eat a mouthful of pork as a symbol of renouncing the covenant (see 2 Macc 6:18—7:42). These martyrs served as notable examples of commitment to God and Torah in Hellenistic Judaism (see 2 Macc 6:28, 31; 4 Macc 1.8). The martyrs' experience, like Jesus' crucifixion, involved not only extreme physical pain, but also complete degradation. The physical violation of the person assaulted the person's honor, and his or her death cut off any possibility for the reparation of honor in this life. Pain and shame were intentionally joined (cf. Heb 12:2), as seen in the mocking, scornful atmosphere of the tortures (2 Macc 7:7, 10). Like Jesus, they endure the pain and do not allow the experience of disgrace to weaken their commitment to God and their resolve to remain obedient. The author makes it clear that they had a way out, indeed a way back to a comfortable and even enviable life according to Antiochus's offer of personal patronage (2 Macc 7:24; 4 Macc 8:5–7). Like Abraham, they had the opportunity to abandon the journey where faith led, but they persevered in order to obtain the reward of "a better resurrection."[16] In the eyes of the Hellenizers they appear to be acting irrationally and dishonorably, spurning the good of enfranchisement in the new "Greek" Jerusalem. In their own eyes (and, they assure themselves, in God's eyes), resistance

16. The martyrs seek a "better" resurrection in comparison with the temporary resuscitation (i.e., the return to the life of *this* world) of the sons of women such as the widows in Zarephath and Shunem (Heb 11:35a; see 1 Kgs 17:17–24; 2 Kgs 4:8–37). Throughout Hebrews, whatever pertains to life in the world to come is "better" than the life and enjoyments of this world (see 10:34; 11:16).

and endurance of disgraceful treatment preserves their integrity and honor before the court of God and the community of faith (4 Macc 13:17; 17:5, 20).

The Maccabean martyrs lead an unnumbered host of people who suffered a variety of martyrdoms, physical abuse, and forms of social dislocation for their commitment to God (11:36–38). These were all marginalized in the extreme, enjoying no place in society, subject to every form of disgrace at society's hands. Some experienced this through the deviancy-control mechanisms of imprisonment, corporeal punishment, and public execution.[17] Others were pushed to the extreme margins of the dominant society, and beyond the margins— living in the hills, dressing themselves in animal skins rather than the accouterments of civilization (e.g., spun cloth).[18] For the sake of persevering in faithful response to God, they have renounced their place in the larger society and accepted the loss of all status in that society. This again connects with the experience of at least some in the community who had been deprived of their property and thus, depending on the extent of this confiscation, of their protection from the shame of penury. The author will later exhort his audience to "leave the camp" (in terms of any sense of belonging, rootedness, or ambition for acceptance, rather than physical removal),

17. The author's descriptions of these executions specifically recall traditions about the executions of Isaiah, Jeremiah, and Ezekiel also found in *Lives of the Prophets* and *Martyrdom of Isaiah*.

18. On clothing as indicative of social status, see Neyrey, "Loss of Wealth," 136. Wandering as opposed to a settled life within the lines of the social order "replicates the social behavior that rejects ascribed status and implies a willingness to be deviant within the broader context. Yet the willingness to be deviant itself becomes a value worthy of honor within the group" (Malina and Neyrey, "Honor and Shame," 27).

figuratively replicating the existence of those who left behind the "civilized" spaces to live a homeless existence in deserts and caves (13:12–14).

The author introduces a striking remark into the middle of this list of those who were shamed and marginalized by the dominant society: "the world was not worthy of them" (11:38). The author turns the larger society's norms and evaluations of honor and disgrace upside down: the honor or value of the person of "faith" is not measured by the standards of the society; rather, that society's honor (or lack thereof) is measured by the standard of the faithful and by the standard of how it has treated the faithful. If the society has shamed the sect, this is a reflection of the society's lack of honor, not the lack of honor of the members of the sect.[19] The audience's neighbors' negative evaluation and rejection of them is, thus, a judgment upon those neighbors.[20] Only those who obey God in "trust" (*pistis*), who secure God as their Patron, who look also to the unseen and future realities when evaluating and making choices, are capable of knowing what is truly

19. The author of Hebrews effects a coup similar to that of Epictetus in his discourse on the Cynic, in which the Cynic becomes the one who evaluates worth and the standard by which others are assessed (*Diss.* 3.22.63, 65).

20. Cf. Epictetus, *Diss.* 1.29.50–54. Epictetus argues that the real issue is not whether or not one has been insulted or censured, but whether one has been censured correctly. If not, the wise person suffers no real injury: "if he had passed judgment upon some hypothetical syllogism and had made a declaration, 'I judge the statement, "If it is day, there is light," to be false,' what has happened to the hypothetical syllogism? Who is being judged in this case, who has been condemned? The hypothetical syllogism, or the man who has been deceived in his judgment about it? . . . Shall the truly educated man pay attention to an uninstructed person when he passes judgment?"

honorable or shameful: it is their critique of the unbelievers that is valid, not the opposite.[21]

The Community's Past Example

The examples of faith all serve to reinforce the community's own past example, which precedes the encomium. Fundamentally, the audience needs to "remember the earlier days" and "not throw away their boldness" and, with it, their attainment of the reward that their past actions have already all but won for them (10:32–36). Speakers were known to appeal to a group's past accomplishments or previous investment in a particular endeavor to encourage the completion of a difficult task once begun. At the climax of Tacitus' *Agricola* (33–34), the Roman general rallies his troops with these words:

> The long road we have traveled, the forests we have threaded our way through, the estuaries we have crossed—all redound to our credit and honor as long as we keep our eyes to the front. . . . I would quote the examples of other armies to encourage you. As things are, you need only recall your own battle-honors, only question your own eyes.

The speaker motivates the hearers first by rousing confidence: just as the army succeeded in its former campaigns, which were not unlike the present challenge, so it would succeed again. The speaker also subtly arouses fear—the army's former achievements and glory would come to nothing should they fail to succeed in the present challenge.[22] The author of

21. Cf. 4 Macc 11.4–6; 12:11, 13.

22. See also Dio, *Philoct.* (*Or.* 59.2): "This thirst for glory [*philotimia*] leads me to . . . accept every fresh peril, fearing to mar the glory won by earlier achievements."

Hebrews harnesses the double edge of this device, drawing the addressees' attention to their former endurance and faithful action, intensifying its power by pointing out the nearness of the goal for which they have been striving and sacrificing all along (10:35–36). It is a mark of honor for them to continue in, and a mark of dishonor to abandon, their former course.

The "contest" that the author recalls for the audience involved disgrace and loss of status, and the addressees are praised precisely for enduring dishonor (10:32). The author challenges them to continue to endure this social pressure, resisting the temptation to "shrink back" from open identification with the sect by assimilating again into their old social networks and practices. They are urged to continue to manifest *parrhēsia*, a word frequently translated "confidence," but indicating something more forceful here. As this word is elsewhere an antonym of "shame" (*aischunē*, Phil 1:20; 1 John 2:28), so here it should be heard as the opposite of sensitivity to the larger society's opinion. The community had been "bold" in the face of their neighbors' disapproval and sanctions of reproach and punishment. They had been "outspoken" about their commitment to Jesus and his people in their speech and actions.[23] They are called to continue in that "boldness" rather than "shrink back" in shame before their neighbors, yielding to their social pressure. Written into the community's own past endurance is the faith of Abraham, who relinquished his status in his homeland in order to attain new status as a citizen of God's city, the faith of Moses, who chose disgrace and abuse in solidarity with God's people over ease and honor apart from them (thus, in "sin"), and the faith of the martyrs

23. On *parrhēsia* as "outspokenness," see 4 Macc 10:1–5; deSilva, *4 Maccabees*, 184–85.

and marginalized, who left the safe spaces of society and suffered degradation in the present for the sake of an honorable eternity. The audience is thus encouraged to persevere in their former faith and commitment (*pistis*), and assured that, if they do, they will exchange their temporary dishonor in the sight of the world for eternal honor before God.

Reinterpreting Experiences of Social Shame

While on the one hand encouraging the Christians to accept it as a normal pattern that seeking honor before God and God's benefits entails moving into the places of lower status and even disgrace in the eyes of the dominant society, the author also works to reinterpret their experiences of disgrace at the hands of the dominant society in ways that are ennobling, thus removing the sting of those experiences. By attaching positive significance to these experiences from within the alternative culture's worldview, the author seeks not only to undermine the dominant society's attempts at social control (i.e., their quest to shame the "deviants" back into conformity with society's norms), but even to make these same experiences an occasion for strengthening commitment to the minority culture by turning the experiences of disgrace into tokens of honor and promises of greater reward.

One important interpretive lens that the author holds up to the believers' experiences of ridicule, trial, loss of status and property, and their endurance of continued reproach is the lens of the rigors of education, particularly God's training or discipline of God's adopted children. The interpretive frame "works" insofar as formative discipline normally entails enduring that which is unpleasant, and often that which is experienced as shaming. Nevertheless, within this frame, the experiences are not themselves ultimately degrading, but rather are formative for an honorable and privileged future. The community's endurance of society's rejection and censure turns out to be the token of God's acceptance and the process of formative discipline whereby the addressees are fitted to receive their birthright and to enjoy the honor toward which God is leading them (2:10):

> You have forgotten the exhortation that addresses you as sons and daughters:

> "My child, do not regard lightly the formative discipline [*paideia*] of the Lord,
> nor lose courage while being reproved by him.
> For whom the Lord loves, he disciplines,
> and chastens every child whom he receives."

> Endure for the sake of formative discipline: God is treating you as children, for who is the child whom a father does not discipline? If you are without the formative discipline that all [children] share, then you are bastards and not legitimate children. Since we have had our biological fathers as educators and showed reverence, shall we not much more be subject to the Father of spirits and live? For they disciplined us for a few days as seemed best to them, but he [disciplines us] for our benefit, that we may share his holiness. All formative discipline [*paideia*], while it is present, does not seem to be joyful, but grievous; but later it yields the peaceful fruit [*karpon*] of righteousness to those who have been trained through it. (12:5–11)

The author invites the believers to view their struggle to hold onto their confession in the face of society's hostility and censure as their endurance in *paideia*, the "education" or "formative discipline" by means of which all parents mold their children's character and prepare them for productive futures. The social pressures that society intends as experiences of disgrace aimed at bringing the deviant back into line with the values of the dominant culture become the proof of the believers' adoption into God's family and a powerful encouragement to persevere in their commitments to the minority group. Only those who have shared in such discipline (12:8) will also share the rewards as "partners of Christ" (3:14) and "partners in a heavenly calling" (3:1). The believers may even cherish their marginalization and censure by society as a process by which their character is tried and proven, and which guarantees their future honor and vindication.[24] This interpretive lens, the readers will recall from chapter 1, was also known in Greco-Roman philosophical discourse (see Seneca, *Prov.*).

A second interpretive lens that the author uses is the metaphor of the athletic contest (the *agōn*) when he speaks of the traumatic experience of public disgrace and social and economic disenfranchisement suffered by the believers (10:32–34). The author invites the audience to view themselves not as victims, but as contenders, summing up their experience as a "competition" or "contest" (*athlēsis*). The fifth-century bishop John Chrysostom, himself a part of the ancient Mediterranean honor culture, recognized the rhetorical force of this metaphor: the author "did not say 'trials' but

24. The author of Wis 3:5 uses the same interpretive frame, looking afresh at the shameful death suffered on behalf of righteousness as the divine discipline by which God tests and proves the worth of an individual and fits him or her to become the recipient of God's eternal benefits.

'contest' [*athlēsis*], which is an expression of commendation and of very great praise."[25] The metaphor positions the audience to look at the experience of shame and abuse, and at their neighbors' agenda, quite differently: these neighbors are competitors seeking to defeat the converts in their purposes, to bring them down not by the attempts to shame them, but by getting them to capitulate and admit defeat in the face of such tactics. By contending and persevering, then, they have in fact contended nobly and, in effect, won the first round.

A more extended use of this athletic imagery appears in the exhortation built around the example of Jesus:

> Having, therefore, such a great cloud of spectators surrounding us, let us also run with endurance the racing course [*agōn*] laid out before us, putting off every weight and the sin which so easily trips us up, looking away to faith's pioneer and perfecter—Jesus, who, for the sake of the joy set before him, endured a cross, despising shame, and has sat down at the right hand of God's throne. Consider him who had endured from sinners such hostility against himself, in order that you may not become faint, growing weary in your souls. You have not yet, while contending in the ring [*antagōnizomenoi*] against sin, fought back to the point of spilling your own blood. (12:1–4)

The heroes of faith whose "witness" to God the author has just recalled at length have become an "encircling crowd of spectators" watching how the audience will now compete against the same social forces that they, in their generations, defeated for the sake of the prizes offered by God. The author directs

25. Chrysostom, *Com. Heb.* 10:32, NPNF1 14:461; Migne, PG 63.149.

the audience's gaze to this court of opinion as a worthy group from which to seek honor and esteem. Like those who compete in races, the believers are to "lay aside" everything that might impede their running: they are to set aside "sin" as if it were a close-fitting garment that restricted their movement toward the prize and threatened to trip them up as they ran. As runners clear their minds of all distractions and set their eyes wholly toward the goal, so the believers are to fix their gaze on Jesus, who has run ahead to the victory in which all may share (12:2), if they keep running (that is, continue forward in the direction in which they began to move decisively in their conversion). Shifting images a bit from running to wrestling, the author says that they are contending against sin, their antagonist in this contest.

Athletic competitions held a great appeal in an honor culture such as the Hellenistic and Roman world, affording the victors in the various events an opportunity for achieving fame and esteem. Spokespersons of minority cultures quickly turned to athletics as a field of metaphors that they could use to set the disgrace and abuse suffered by their members (which parallel the rigors of athletic training and the hardships endured in the ring) in the light of an honorable competition for victory.[26] Philosophers such as Epictetus make extensive use of athletic imagery, recasting the struggle against hardships or the reproach of outsiders as a wrestling match in which the philosopher who endures is promised an honorable victory (cf. *Diss.* 1.24.1–2; 1.18.21). Both Epictetus and Dio Chrysostom speak of the life of the Cynic philosopher as an athletic contest. Although the Cynic deliberately seeks to

26. For a detailed discussion, see Pfitzner, *Paul and the Agon Motif*; Croy, *Endurance*, 37–70.

place himself outside of society's evaluation, seeking the margins and extremes of human existence, his life is a veritable "Olympic contest" (Epictetus, *Diss.* 3.22.52). The hardships he suffers, such as sleeping out of doors, going hungry, and other straits that are interpreted by members of the dominant culture as signs of a depraved and disgraceful existence, are interpreted from within the minority culture as divine training by Zeus to overcome weaknesses of character (*Diss.* 3.22.56) and as participation in a noble competition for virtue (Dio, *Or.* 8.11–13).

Jewish authors put athletic imagery to similar use, again as an image by which to turn the degradation and suffering occasionally inflicted upon faithful Jews into a competition for honor before God. The question becomes no longer "How can I live with this shame?" but, rather, "Am I going to let this aggressor deprive me of the honor that God bestows on those who contend bravely for God's sake?" 4 Maccabees speaks of a series of executions—the shameful death of deviants, as far as members of the dominant culture would be concerned— as just such a quest. The seven brothers who die under the tortures that strip them of their honor and status as surely as they strip them of their flesh are praised as "athletes" (*askētas*) and competitors (*agōnistai*, 12:15); their tortures become a contest (*agōn*), the Gentile king's court an "arena" (*gymnasia*, 11:20). The disgrace of punishment and mutilation becomes a "noble contest" in which they contend on behalf of the honor of their ancestral law (16:16). Near the work's conclusion, the author summarizes the narrative within an extended athletic metaphor comparable in scope to Heb 12:1–4:

> Truly it was a divine contest. Virtue was offering
> the prize, examining them by means of endurance.

> Victory meant imperishability in an aeon-long
> life. Eleazar contended first, and the mother of
> the seven children joined the competition, and
> the seven brothers were competing. They were
> matched against the tyrant in the competition, and
> the world and the manner of living of human be-
> ings were looking on. Reverence for God won the
> victory, crowning her own athletes. Who did not
> admire the athletes of the divinely given law? Who
> was not astounded? (4 Macc 17:11–16)

The author of Hebrews thus applies a firmly established
tradition to the needs of his audience, recasting them in such
a way that persistence against the contrary social forces,
rather than acquiescence to the same, is the true path to
honor. The response that would lead to restoration of honor
and approval from the larger society is recast, strategically,
as a response that signals defeat (not recovery). Interpreting
the addressees' experience as a contest allows the author to
harness the widely praised virtue of courage, and to define the
courageous path as perseverance or "endurance" in Christian
community and activity. Endurance is prominent in classical discussions of the virtue of courage (cf. *Rhet. Her.* 3.2.3:
"courage is . . . the endurance of hardship in expectation of
profit") and in the author's exhortation. As Jesus endured
both cross and contradiction (12:2–3), so the addressees are
called to endure in their contest (12:1) and in God's training
(12:7). The author ennobles the audience's experience of dishonor and rejection at society's hands, the price of their perseverance in the sect, as a manifestation of this noble virtue.

As competitors matched against a powerful contender
(the larger society's representatives) and who have endured

this contender's fury, the converts are no longer victims, but victors. Though the competition has cost them significantly, they are not "losers" for having endured, but the winners, whose victory at the end of a strenuous competition would be applauded by those who themselves knew the rigors of the contest and had been victorious, and by the God for whose honor they persevered. They follow thus in the praiseworthy example of Jesus, who competed ahead of them and for them, and who was exalted to the honor of being seated at God's right hand after his successful competition. His example gives them further assurance that their own "contest" will result in honor before God.

CONCLUSION

An important facet of the author's strategy for meeting the challenges of his audience's situation involves elevating as "honorable" (and, therefore, fit objects for emulation) those who have, for the sake of pursuing goals consistent with the goals of the sect, set aside the larger society's negative evaluation of them and the social pressure of shaming its members could apply. A notable feature of the examples of Abraham and the martyrs, as the author has strategically crafted these examples, is the refusal to *return* to a place of at-homeness in the society that they left behind, a determination to endure rather than to diminish the tension existing between them and the larger society.

The believers have lost their place in their homeland for the sake of God's promise, and, like Abraham, are not to grow weary and turn back from their pilgrimage in order to regain that lost status. Rather, they are to embrace life in the margins of society (and thus remain committed to their identity as a sectarian body): "let us go forth to [Jesus] outside the camp and bear the abuse he endured," seeking "the city that is to come" (13:12–14). Like the martyrs and the marginalized, they are not to seek to reduce the tension between themselves and the dominant culture, or to recover a "home" within the society, because of their commitment to God. Like Moses, they are to choose solidarity with the people of God, even at the cost of exclusion from the pleasurable enjoyments of honor and wealth which society offers to its own faithful, devoting themselves to the ongoing life of the sect through assembling together for mutual support (10:25) and caring for those who have been particularly singled out by society for punishment (13:3).

The audience finds themselves at a place where reducing sectarian tension with their neighbors has been an attractive option for some members (10:25); the author writes to counter any lingering tendencies in this direction. Insulating them against a returning sensitivity to society's means of enforcing adherence to its self-preserving values and goals (that is, reinforcing their ability to "despise shame") is prerequisite to their ability to continue on in a course of ongoing tension with, and potentially hostility from, the host society. The author encourages them in this perseverance by drawing their attention to the honor that "faith" and "faithful" action brings in the sight of God and the community of God's people, as well as the ultimate reward of enfranchisement in a better, eternal homeland. In light of this greater goal, the experiences of social pressure can be engaged as a contest in which the audience will come out as "winners" by not yielding to those pressures (thus, being willing to be treated as "losers" by their neighbors), or as a process of formative discipline that tests and purifies their commitment to, and embodiment of, the values of the sect—a process that will ultimately lead to the recognition of their value and honor before God. Where it becomes a mark of "honor" before God to suffer "disgrace" from outsiders on account of commitment to the group, the society's ability to effectively apply social pressure and erode commitment to the sect is severely compromised.[27]

27. Compare the similar reversal of values in Acts 5:41, where the apostles, having been scourged as a sign of the authorities' disapproval, "celebrated the fact that they were judged worthy to suffer dishonor for the sake of the name [of Jesus]."

FOUR

Sociorhetorical Strategy II: Grace and Reciprocity in Hebrews

In this chapter, we turn to another principal strategy that the author employs "to motivate and persuade the audience."[1] The author employs the roles, scripts, and ethic of a foundational social institution—the institution of reciprocal relationships, whether patronage or friendship—to reinforce a fundamental facet of the sect's world construction (the relationship forged between God and the members of the sect through Jesus, the focal figure, who also serves to differentiate the Christian sect from other Jewish groups) and, thereby, motivate ongoing adherence to the sect against social pressures to the contrary. Powerful sanctions exist in the audience's environment, and thus in their primary socialization, reinforcing the necessity of making a grateful response to one's benefactors and steering one forcefully away from any response that can be considered

1. Elliott, *Social-Scientific Criticism*, 11.

ungrateful. Persistent and pervasive appeal is made to these sanctions throughout the author's letter.

John Elliott writes that "the acid test to be applied to all the conclusions of literary and historical critics of the Bible is to ask the questions, Did people really think and act that way and, if so, why? Do these exegetical conclusions square with ancient patterns of belief and behavior?" Do the conclusions of exegetes concerning the text in fact cohere "with the actual perceptions, values, worldviews, and social scripts of the communities in which these texts originated?"[2] In this chapter we will devote considerable space to examining a particular ancient "pattern of behavior" and its associated "values and social scripts" as the basis for analyzing an overarching ideological strategy on the part of the author of Hebrews as he reinterprets the audience's situation in terms of assessing the value of, and honorable response to, benefits received.

This ideological strategy is indeed a bold one. The author presents what the audience has received as a result of joining the Christian community, what they've experienced as part of the life of this community, and what they've been *told* they've received (but of which they have no first-hand experience) all as gifts and privileges bestowed upon them by God, their divine patron. The author harnesses the roles and expectations of patron-client relationships, a fundamental social institution of the Hellenistic and Roman periods, to speak of the divine-human relationship in an effort to reorient the audience towards their experience in the sect in a way that will nurture steadfastness within their new social networks. He urges the audience to value the favor and the promises

2. Ibid.

they have received from God through the mediation of Jesus. He admonishes them to continue to show gratitude to the divine Giver by remaining loyal to the Son and to the people whom God has called together in the Son, by continuing to bear positive witness to the value of God's favor and gifts through continued "confession" of their relationship with the Son, and by continuing willingly to suffer loss for the sake of maintaining this relationship in testimony to the surpassing value of what that relationship has brought them. This particular ideological strategy serves the author's social agenda very directly: the path of showing gratitude toward God is the path that leads to continued investment in, and identification with, the Christian sect, and, hence, continued resistance of any and all social pressure applied by members of other, more powerful groups within the larger society to members of the sect to return to their former social networks and practices.

The Social Context of "Grace"

God's beneficence, responding to God's favor, and the causal connection between the two provide the pulse of the sermon "to the Hebrews." At numerous points throughout the sermon, the author speaks of the gifts or gracious actions of God or of Jesus that the hearers have enjoyed as a result of responding positively to the Christian proclamation and joining the Christian community. They have received:

- freedom from the fear of death and from the slavery that such fear brings (2:14–15);
- the "help" of so powerful and exalted a figure as the Son of God (2:16–18);

- the mediation of a sympathetic, "great high priest" who can unfailingly secure timely aid from God for the audience (4:14–16; 7:26–28; etc.);
- the gifts of "having once been enlightened, having tasted the heavenly gift, having received a share of the Holy Spirit, and having tasted the goodness of the word of God and the powers of the age to come" (6:4–5);
- a secure hope in God that provides "a sure and steadfast anchor for the soul" (6:19);
- the removal of the defilement of sin from their conscience *and* from the memory of God, the decisive cleansing that fits them to stand in God's real presence (8:7—10:18);
- the promise of entrance into God's place of rest (4:1), a heavenly homeland (11:16), abiding city (Heb 13:14), unshakable kingdom (12:28), "heaven itself" (9:24), the divine realm beyond the visible heavens, into which Jesus has already entered as their forerunner (6:19–20), where they would enjoy the "better and lasting possessions" kept for them in the abiding realm (10:34).

Alongside the frequent naming of such divine benefits, the author frequently speaks about human response to God, often with some implicit connection to a particular gracious provision of God or of the Son:

- "How will we escape if we neglect so great a provision for deliverance?!" (2:3);

- "Watch out, brothers and sisters, lest there be in any among you a wicked, distrustful heart that turns away from the living God!" (3:12);

- "Let us fear lest, while the promise to enter into God's rest remains, any of you think it fitting to stop short of it" (4:1);

- "Since we have such a great high priest, . . . let us draw near to the throne of favor with boldness, in order that we may receive mercy and find favor for timely help" (4:14–16);

- "Don't become sluggish, but rather become imitators of those who, through patient trust, inherit what God has promised" (6:12);

- "Since we have boldness to enter the Holy Places through the blood of Jesus, . . . let us hold onto the profession of our hope without wavering, because the One who promised is reliable, and let us consider one another unto an outpouring of love and good works, not neglecting our assembling together, as is the habit of some, but encouraging one another— and this all the more as you see the Day drawing near!" (10:19–25);

- "Don't throw away your boldness, for it holds a great reward" (10:35);

- "Don't be immoral or godless like Esau, who gave away his birthright for a single meal" (12:16);

- "Since we are receiving an unshakable kingdom, let us show gratitude, through which we will serve God in a manner pleasing to him with reverence and godly fear" (12:28).

- "Jesus suffered outside the gates in order to conse-
  crate the people through his own blood; therefore
  let us go out to him outside the camp, carrying the
  disgrace he bore" (13:12–13).

The author devotes much of his sermon to calling attention to the gifts that God has provided or promised, the access
to God's favor that the Son has secured for the congregation,
the help that the Son continues to give, and the costly means
by which all of these good things have been made available.
He spends a great deal of the balance of the sermon instruct-
ing the congregation on how to respond to these gifts and acts
of favor. At key points in the sermon,[3] the causal nexus between gift and response is explicitly expressed: "*Since* we have
such a great high priest, . . . *let us* . . ." (4:14, 16); "*Since* we have
boldness to enter the Holy Places through the blood of Jesus,
. . . *let us* . . ." (10:19, 23); "*Since* we are receiving an unshakable kingdom, *let us show gratitude* . . ." (12:28). The author
appears to be trying to direct the audience to make an appropriate response to the gifts and privileges they have received,
and indeed to foreground this dynamic of responding to God's
beneficence in his audience's decision making process.

Undergirding the whole of this sermon is the socially
learned logic of reciprocity that formed the bedrock of the traditional, preindustrial societies of the classical and Hellenistic
world within which the Christian proclamation and the
Christian movement itself took shape. We are accustomed

3. George Guthrie has shown the structural importance of 4:14–16
and 10:19–22 as principal transitional sections in the sermon (*Structure
of Hebrews*, 79–82, 144). 12:28 is a kind of summative exhortation
growing from an argument that itself sums up a great deal of the argumentation of Hebrews (12:25–27).

to look to specific texts from the Jewish Scriptures when we want to dig into the background of an early Christian text like Hebrews, but there are other formative backgrounds as well, for example, the background of social institutions, interactions, and scripts. The latter can be every bit as formative as the Jewish Scriptures themselves, since they are embedded just as deeply if not more deeply in the consciousness of people raised in the midst of those social institutions, interactions, and scripts.[4]

Social-scientific interpretation involves looking closely at relevant social institutions to which an author refers, upon whose "rules" and roles he or she draws while framing his or her strategically crafted response to the audience and their social situation. In this way, the modern interpreter can hear the text's implications and incentives more fully, having sensitized himself or herself to the "social logic" and cultural codes that the text invokes. In regard to Hebrews, this means, first and foremost, searching out the social context of the language of "grace" and its related concepts, a social-semantic domain upon which the author frequently draws.

The author of Hebrews, like other New Testament authors, speaks much about "grace" (in Greek, *charis*):

4. The Jewish Scriptures are an essential ideological background for all the New Testament writers, providing a basic cosmic framework, a broad matrix of stories that are mapped onto the narrative of the early Christians, a vision of God and of the identity of the people of God in the world. But the Greco-Roman social environment is a primary background *experientially and practically* for most New Testament authors and audiences—certainly for any intended audience of literature emanating from or to the mission fields beyond Palestine (e.g., Luke-Acts, the Pauline letters, Hebrews, 1 Peter, Revelation). These audiences lived within, observed, participated in, and fully internalized facets of the Greco-Roman social environment every day of their lives.

We see the one who was for a little while made lower than the angels—Jesus, crowned with glory and honor on account of having suffered death, so that by God's grace [*charis*] he might taste death for everyone. (2:9)

Let us boldly approach the throne of grace [*charis*], in order that we may receive mercy and find grace [*charis*] for timely help. (4:16)

Of how much worse punishment, do you think, will this one be judged worthy—the one who has trampled the Son of God under foot, and has treated as ordinary the blood of the covenant by which he was sanctified, and has outraged the Spirit of grace [*charis*]? (10:29)

See to it that no one falls short of God's grace [*charis*]. (12:15)

Since we are receiving a kingdom that can't be shaken, let us show gratitude ["let us have *charis*"]. (12:28)

Don't be carried off by diverse and foreign teachings, for it is a fine thing for one's heart to be made firm by grace [*charis*], and not by foods that have not benefitted those who are involved with them (13:9).

Grace [*charis*] be with you all. (13:25).

As we try to hear the sermon with all the force and the nuances with which the first audience would have experienced it, that is, in line with how they "really thought and acted," we need to ask some important questions:

1. Where would "grace" language be at home in their everyday world? Where would the hearers have been exposed to this language, perhaps regularly and repeatedly, beyond the assembly gathered in the early Christian house church to hear the text being read?

2. What information or presuppositions will the hearers bring to the hearing of this text from those other settings?

3. To what extent does the author seek to challenge or correct the presuppositions or experience that the hearers may bring to their interpretation of the text, and to what extent does the author depend on, assume, and build upon the knowledge or experience the hearers are bringing?

Classical and Hellenistic Greek authors place this word squarely within the social-semantic field of patronage and clientage. The multivalence of the word is striking. *Charis* could denote, first, the willingness of a patron or friend to grant help of some kind. Aristotle, for example, defines *charis* as the disposition of a benefactor "to render a service to one who needs it" (*Rhet.* 2.7.2). The same word could denote, secondly, the actual help or gifts conferred, as in 2 Cor 8:19 where Paul speaks of the "generous gift" he is administering (namely, the collection being taken up for the church in Jerusalem). *Charis* is used, thirdly, to denote the proper response to a benefactor or friend and his or her gifts, namely "gratitude," as when Dio Chrysostom exclaims, "What is more sacred than honor or gratitude [*charis*]?" in the midst of an oration taking a city to task for failing to show proper and lasting gratitude and honor towards its public benefactors (*Or.* 31.37). "Grace" (*charis*) was the keyword within the ancient social systems of friendship, patronage, and benefaction.[5]

Most literary texts from the Hellenistic and Roman periods are "high-context documents," that is, texts that presume a great deal of shared cultural and social knowledge and "codes" between author and audience. To understand such texts without importing anachronistic or ethnocentric presuppositions, the modern reader needs to work hard to gain the necessary knowledge about the social and cultural context that the author and the audience shared, so as to hear the texts as "insiders." There are texts that go out of their way, as it were, to let the reader in and to help him or her follow the discussion. Seneca's *On Benefits* (*De beneficiis*), for example, takes as its object of exploration a code of conduct—the giving, receiving, and returning of favors. The code of conduct that other documents might presume is here given meticulous, explicit attention. It does not presume insider debates, but illustrates precisely what those debates are and how the different positions might play out in real-life interactions. It is a monologue that operates at a meta-level *above* social interactions, not presuming the dynamics at work in everyday speech and interaction, but purposefully laying those dynamics bare to view and examination. The classical rhetorical handbooks and much ethical literature (for example, Aristotle's *Nicomachean Ethics*, or collections of advice from both Jewish and non-Jewish authors) operate similarly, explaining the codes that, in daily interaction or speech, might otherwise be presumed. Such texts provide access, as it were,

5. For a fuller introduction to this social institution and its associated ethic, and its importance for New Testament interpretation, see deSilva, *Honor, Patronage*, 95–156.

to native informants, helping modern readers enter into those social systems and construct the models that would be required for reading higher-context documents like Hebrews, in which the social values and scripts of patronage and reciprocity, for example, are indeed presumed but not explicated. In other words, these are the sorts of texts that can help us answer reliably the question, "Did people really think and act that way and, if so, why?"[6]

The giving and receiving of aid and benefactions between friends or between patrons and clients was, according to Seneca, "the practice that constitutes the chief bond of human society" (*Ben.* 1.4.2).[7] The Greco-Roman world was held together by social networks of favor and loyalty. The system did not lend itself to precise evaluations of favors exchanged, such that mutual commitment tended to be long-term. The point of the institution was not even exchange, but ongoing exchange. Mutual bonds of favor and obligation provided the glue that maintained social cohesion. In such a society, gratitude becomes an essential virtue, and ingratitude the "cardinal social and political sin" (*Ben.* 7.31.1).

In a world in which wealth and property were concentrated into the hands of a very small percentage of the population, the majority of people often found themselves in need of assistance in one form or another, and therefore had to seek the patronage of those who were better placed in

6. Elliott, *Social-Scientific Criticism*, 11.

7. Patronage took two principal forms in the ancient world: public and personal. Inscriptions throughout the Mediterranean world attest to the response of gratitude made by a city, a guild, or some other group to a public benefactor, showing that the basic logic of reciprocity held true. We are concerned here, however, more with personal patronage and the long-term relational bonds formed thereby.

the world than themselves. Patrons might be asked to provide money, grain, employment, or land; the better-connected persons could be sought out as patrons for the opportunities they would give for professional or social advancement (see Seneca, *Ben.* 1.2.4). One who received such a benefit became a client to the patron, accepting the obligation to publicize the favor and his or her gratitude for it, thus contributing to the patron's reputation. The client also accepted the obligation of loyalty to a patron and could be called upon to perform services for the patron, thus contributing to the patron's power. The reception of a gift and the acceptance of the obligation of gratitude are inseparable.

Sometimes the most important gift that a friend or patron could give would be access to another patron within his or her own network. When I cannot get what I need or want through my immediate network of friends and patrons, the question becomes, "Who can connect me with the person who can grant me the assistance I need or desire?" Modern anthropologists call such a person a "broker," but the ancients had a word for such a person as well—"mediator" (in Greek, *mesitēs*). Brokerage or mediation was exceedingly common and personal in the ancient world. The letters of Pliny the Younger, governor of Bithynia around 110 CE, to the emperor Trajan, for example, document Pliny's attempts to gain imperial benefactions for Pliny's own friends and clients. The gift of access to Trajan's favor was itself a tremendous gift that further bound Pliny's clients to himself.[8]

---

8. De Ste. Croix ("Suffragium") cites numerous examples of brokerage from the letters of Cicero (first century BCE), Pliny (late first to early second century CE), and Fronto (second century CE). See also deSilva, *Honor, Patronage*, 97–99.

It is also quite significant that Greeks, Romans, and Jews all used social relationships that they could observe among people whom they *could* see to talk about their relationships with the divine, whom they could *not* see. Not surprisingly, the model of clients to a great Patron is prominent in such discussions, whether one is reading Aristotle, Seneca, Epictetus, Philo, or 4 Maccabees.[9] Priests were often regarded as mediators, or "brokers," between the divine and humanity. Indeed, the Latin word for priest—*pontifex*—comes from two morphemes meaning "bridge" and "builder." Gods and human patrons stood along a continuum: the quality of the gifts might be radically different, the givers ontologically different, but the nature and dynamics of the relationships were of a kind, resting along a continuum, as it were. As one moved further along this continuum, the possibility of ever fully returning the favor became more remote, and the generosity and graciousness inherent in the giving approached the perfection and freedom that was the ideal for all givers.[10] But it was still a continuum.

The trinity of senses held together by the one word *charis* —generous disposition, gift, and grateful response—already suggests implicitly what many moralists from the Greek and Roman cultures stated explicitly: "grace" must be met with "grace," favor must always give birth to favor (cf. Sophocles, *Ajax* 522), gift must always be met with gratitude. The person who accepted a benefaction in the ancient world simultaneously accepted the obligation to show gratitude. In Seneca's

9. This is reflected also, for example, in the adoption of "patron deities" by individuals and collectives (e.g., guilds or cities). See Saller, *Patronage*, 23.

10. See Aristotle, *Eth. nic.* 8.14.3–4; Seneca, *Ben.* 4.26.1; 4.28.1; 7.31.4.

words, "the person who intends to be grateful, immediately while receiving, should turn his or her thought to repaying" (*Ben.* 2.25.3).

This ethos was visually depicted in the popular image of the three "Graces," three goddesses dancing hand in hand in a circle. Seneca interprets this image thus: there are three graces, since "there is one for bestowing a benefit, one for receiving it, and a third for returning it." They dance hand in hand because "a benefit passing in its course from hand to hand returns nevertheless to the giver; the beauty of the whole is destroyed if the course is anywhere broken, and it has most beauty if it is continuous and maintains an uninterrupted succession" (*Ben.* 1.3.2–5).[11] There ought not to be such a thing as an isolated act of "grace." An act of favor initiates a circle dance in which the recipients of favor must "return the favor," that is, give again to the giver (both in terms of a generous disposition and in terms of some gift, whether material or otherwise). Only a gift requited is a gift well and nobly received.[12] Depicting the facets of the grace relationship as goddesses also communicated the sanctity of the relationship: showing gratitude was considered a sacred obligation, while ingratitude was ranked alongside sacrilege (Dio, *Or.* 31.37). "To fail to return grati-

---

11. In extant representations from late antiquity (for example, a famous fresco from Pompeii currently in the Naples Museum), these graces are often depicted not as dancing hand in hand, but holding something in one hand (such as a sprig of laurel) and touching another "grace" with the second hand. They are still represented as standing or moving in a circle, with one grace facing the other two, with hands or arms interwoven. Nevertheless, it is likely that Seneca accurately describes an image readily available to himself and his reader.

12. See, further, deSilva, *Honor, Patronage*, 104–6.

tude is a disgrace," said Seneca, "and the whole world counts it as such" (*Ben.* 3.1.1).

How was gratitude to be expressed or manifested? One prominent component of this response was to bring honor to the benefactor through one's own demeanor and through one's testimony to the generosity and virtue of the benefactor. Aristotle spoke of "honor" as "the due reward for virtue and beneficence" (*Eth. nic.* 8.14.2). Or in Seneca's words, "Let us show how grateful we are for the blessing that has come to us by pouring forth our feelings, and let us bear witness to them, not merely in the hearing of the giver, but everywhere" (*Ben.* 2.22.1; see also 2.24.2). He sternly warns that one should never accept a gift if one would be ashamed to acknowledge the debt publicly; a gift should be accepted only if the recipient were willing to "invite the whole city to witness it" (*Ben.* 2.23.1). One party would thus enjoy the benefit itself, the other party the "prestige" that came from "the ability to confer services which were highly valued and could not be remunerated."[13]

Gratitude involves more than a subjective feeling and more than words. The recipient of a favor seeks opportunities to be of service to the patron, and should place loyalty to the patron above any considerations of personal advantage. According to Seneca, "it is the ungrateful person who thinks: 'I should have liked to return gratitude, but I fear the expense, I fear the danger, I shrink from giving offense; I would rather consult my own interest'" (*Ben.* 4.24.2). He provides a powerful picture of the intense bond that gratitude ought to create:

> No one can be grateful unless he or she has learned
> to scorn the things which drive the common herd

13. Derrett, *Jesus's Audience*, 41. See also Danker, *Benefactor*, 436; and Saller, *Patronage*, 10.

> to distraction; if you wish to make a return for a
> favor, you must be willing to go into exile, or to
> pour forth your blood, or to undergo poverty, or,
> . . . even to let your very innocence be stained and
> exposed to shameful slanders. (*Ep.* 81.27)

Gratitude involves an intense loyalty to the person from whom one has received beneficence, such that one would place a greater value on service to the benefactor than on one's place in one's homeland, one's physical well-being, one's wealth, and one's reputation.

It is important to stress that the logic of reciprocity is *socially learned* logic: it is imprinted through socially observed and socially practiced behavior by means of which first-century people learned about how relationships work, how the world works, what values are part of the very foundation of life together.[14] A child notices how his parents interact with people who have helped the family in some way; he accompanies his father out into the public places and notices how others treat his father with honor, and perhaps asks why. As the child grows, he notices dedicatory inscriptions giving public honors to people who have performed some service or provided private funds for some public building throughout his city, and hears proclamations made declaring new honors for emperor or governor or civic patron. When he receives a favor, those closest to him stimulate his thinking about how to respond, and the importance of responding. And so on. This formative process of social education shapes that child's

---

14. It is *also* reinforced in the literature of the cultures that constitute the Greco-Roman world, including Egyptian, Hebrew, Greek, and Latin literature. The point here, however, is that it is primarily reinforced in daily social interactions and communications.

thinking throughout his adult life; he will bring this knowledge into any new situation where the social dynamics appear to him to be similar.

Another prominent word group in Hebrews is the vocabulary of "faith" or "trust" (*pistis*) and its opposite, "distrust" (*apistia*). These words were also very much at home in patron-client and friendship relations. Like "grace," these words also carry multiple senses. *Pistis* looked to a friend or patron with assurance of that patron's reliability to give what was promised (see Heb 11:6), and in this sense is usually translated as "trust" or "faith." *Pistis* also manifested itself in the client's dependability, "keeping faith" in the sense of showing loyalty and commitment to the patron and to his or her obligations of gratitude.[15] In this context, then, *pistis* speaks to the firmness, reliability, and faithfulness of both parties in the patron-client relationship or the relationship of "friends." Richard Saller observed that "friendship," whether between equals or unequal persons (in the latter case, a patron-client relationship), "was supposed to be founded on virtue (especially *fides*)."[16] It is this *fides*, "faith" or "faithfulness" (*pistis*), to which the author of Hebrews enjoins his readers through both negative and positive models, through warnings and exhortations.

The opposite of *pistis* ("trust," "loyalty") is *apistia*. In one sense, this refers to "distrust" in regard to a patron's or friend's or client's reliability. Distrust springs from a prior, negative evaluation of the character and reliability of the other person, and could be insulting in the extreme if the object of "distrust" were, in fact, a virtuous and trustworthy entity. However, one also had to be prudent when placing

15. This is the sense of "faith" (*pistis*) in 4 Macc 13:13; 16:18–22.

16. Saller, *Patronage*, 12–13.

trust or committing oneself to be relied upon by another (see Dio, *Or.* 73; 74; Seneca, *Ben.* 1.1.2; 4.8.2). *Apistia* could also refer, in its second sense, to "disloyalty" or "unfaithfulness," as when clients fail to remain steadfast in their commitment to their patron or prove untrustworthy in their service. The author of Hebrews foregrounds the dangers of *apistia* both as failure to trust and failure to prove faithful in his most fully developed negative example, that of the exodus generation (see Heb 3:12, 19).

When persons from that world read Hebrews, they encountered a text that spoke of the immense benefits that God had given and more that God promised for the future. They would have encountered a portrayal of Jesus first and foremost as a *mesitēs*, a "mediator" (8:6; 9:15; 12:24) who brings people before God to experience God's favor—God's timely help (Heb 4:14–16). His relationship to God, as "Son," assures successful brokerage. The priestly and sacrificial language does not obscure or displace the essential dynamic that would be evident to all first-century hearers: Jesus stands between human beings in need of God's favor and the God who has all that the human beings could need or want, and Jesus has done and continues to do whatever it takes to connect the people with the experience of God's saving help and the reception of God's eternal promises. According to historian Barbara Levick—and it is indeed interesting to me to find a *Roman* historian also looking at the phenomenon of early Christianity in these terms—Christianity "gave access . . . through an incorruptible intermediary, to a reliable authority, an important offering indeed in a patronal society."[17]

17. Levick, *Government*, 150.

Our ancient audience would also well understand the author's call for a suitable response: "Since we are in the process of receiving an unshakable kingdom, let us show gratitude [*charis*]" (Heb 12:28). The hearers wince at the ungraceful and distrustful responses of the exodus generation or Esau to the privileges accorded them, and shudder at the prospect of making such a response themselves that shows a lack of trust in the Divine Patron regarding the Christian hope and a lack of gratitude for the investment God and God's Son have already made in their deliverance. The author's genius lies in foregrounding this *theological* and *ideological* perspective on the audience's life choices, so that the hearers will continue to choose temporal loss and marginalization in association with the sect rather than abandon the Christian group to sink back into the embrace of the more dominant groups from which they dissociated themselves in their conversion and socialization process.

The Logic of Hebrews 6:1–8 and the Social Logic of Reciprocity

One of the most hotly debated passages in the sermon "to the Hebrews" is 6:4–8, but this debate has rarely taken into account the social logic undergirding the author's argument— the logic that makes this a *compelling* piece of argumentation for this audience. In this section, we will pursue a detailed reading of 6:1–12 as a sample text that is both illumined by the sociocultural context of the author and his audience and uses socially learned codes of behavior as a means of advancing the author's social agenda for the audience in their situation.

Hebrews 6:4–6 confronts the hearer with an argument from the topic of the "impossible," one of the topics common to all genres of rhetoric (cf. Aristotle, *Rhet.* 2.19), in order to provide a rationale (*adunaton gar*, the latter word being used commonly to introduce a rationale for the preceding material) in support of the course of action proposed in 6:1–3, namely moving on to "perfection." In the audience's social situation, moving on to "perfection" means persevering in that enterprise which began with their elementary induction into the values and worldview of the Christian culture, hence persevering in public commitment to and association with the Christian sect. 6:4–6 supports this exhortation by examining the contrary course of action, namely "falling away," the ideologically loaded way in which the author refers to reassimilation into the larger society. The author strategically moves the audience to see no middle ground here: one must *either* press on to the completion of the journey, e.g., by maturing in the faith and taking on a role of responsibility for others in the community, *or* fall away (fall short, shrink back, drift off). This move is grounded in the dominant image he uses to shape the audience's thinking about the Christian life as a pilgrimage: as an exodus from this world and a journey into the eternal homeland. The author further supports the rationale—this argument from the "impossibility" of restoring those who pursue the contrary course of falling away (6:4–6)—with an analogy from agriculture in 6:7–8. This analogy is offered as an explanation (it is also introduced by *gar*) specifically to help the hearer understand why it should be impossible to restore the one who falls away rather than embraces the author's advice to maintain commitment to the group.

How does the shared social knowledge of patronage and reciprocity contribute to leading the audience to accept this "impossibility" as true, as a given? How would they hear this argument, and within what contexts would the argument be persuasive to the hearers? Where would they have encountered similar argumentation and illustrations before?

We begin with the argument from analogy in 6:7–8. In an attempt to search out the background that informs this illustration and can help us hear these verses as the first hearers did, interpreters frequently turn to the Jewish Scriptures. The language of the Scriptures is clearly present. The mention of "thorns and thistles" in connection with a "curse" suggest that the author has drawn upon the language of Gen 3:17–18 in the process of inventing this analogy. The opposition of "blessing" and "curse" recalls at least the general Jewish cultural knowledge of the "curse" and "blessing" in the context of the Deuteronomistic covenant, and may indeed recall Deut 11:26–28 in particular, a text directly concerned with promoting loyalty and obedience toward the God who delivered, and offers to continue to protect and prosper, the covenant people.[18]

Resonances with the social context—with the kind of speech native to the cities in which these Christians lived and moved and had their being—have been largely neglected. Agriculture proved to be a fruitful field for developing illustrations pertinent to patronage. Seneca frequently uses analogies and images drawn from agriculture in his essay on patronage, friendship, and reciprocity. The first cause of the degradation of the system of reciprocity, he asserts, is that "we do not pick out those who are worthy of receiving our gifts. . . . We do not sow seed in worn out and unproductive soil; but our benefits

18. Craddock, "Hebrews," 78; Attridge, *Hebrews*, 173 n. 90.

we give, or rather throw, away without any discrimination" (*Ben.* 1.1.2). This first agricultural metaphor speaks about the quality of the recipient using the analogy of sowing seeds on appropriate soil, namely soil that will produce a good crop rather than prove "worn out and unproductive soil." The same thought is captured later: "we ought to take care to select those to whom we would give benefits, since even the farmer does not commit his seeds to sand" (4.8.2). While Seneca cautions the potential benefactor to choose well the soil in which he or she will plant his or her gifts, "we never wait for absolute certainty [concerning whether or not a recipient will prove grateful], since the discovery of truth is difficult, but follow the path that probable truth shows. All the business of life proceeds in this way. It is thus that we sow . . . for who will promise to the sower a harvest?" (4.33.1–2). The benefactor thus gives with the hope of a harvest of gratitude, but without the certainty of such a harvest. Sowing and harvesting are used here quite naturally as metaphors for giving benefits and enjoying a grateful response from the recipients. Finally, Seneca advises that a single gift may be insufficient to cultivate a client or friend: "The farmer will lose all that he has sown if he ends his labors with putting in the seed; it is only after much care that crops are brought to their yield; nothing that is not encouraged by constant cultivation from the first day to the last ever reaches the stage of fruit. In the case of benefits, the same rule holds" (2.11.4–5).

Nor was such use of agricultural analogies confined to pagan Latin writers. The Jewish author of the *Sentences of Pseudo-Phocylides* writes: "Do no good to a bad person; it is like sowing into the sea" (*Sentences* 152). The "Song of the Vineyard" in Isa 5:1–7 is also worthy of consideration here.

While arguments for the literary *dependence* of Heb 6:7–8 are unconvincing,[19] it remains an apt parallel from the standpoint of the song's dynamics—dynamics explicitly concerned with reciprocity. Isaiah employs an agricultural analogy to illustrate Israel's failure as a people (particularly its elite and empowered) to respond appropriately to divine beneficence, to bring forth the fruits that ought to have followed in response to God's investment of attention, care, and provision for Israel.

These examples suggest that an agricultural illustration would be quite appropriately heard to reinforce some point about fulfilling the obligations of reciprocity, particularly if Heb 6:4–6 articulates a scenario involving patron-client roles and expectations.[20] The upshot of the argument from analogy would be that those who receive gifts—like the soil that receives the gifts of rain and the attention of careful cultivation—ought to bear a suitable return, one that will bring delight to those to whom delight is due, with the result that those people will remain favored. Those who receive these gifts and make an inappropriate return ("thorns and thistles"

19. As in Verbrugge, "Towards a New Interpretation," aptly critiqued by Attridge (*Hebrews*, 172 n. 69). Verbrugge's suggestion that Hebrews 6:4–6 refers to the effects of communal apostasy rather than the individual apostate is difficult to reconcile with the author's concern precisely over "each one" of the congregation (3:12; 4:1; 10:25; 12:15), not the congregation as a collective body.

20. Thompson (*Beginnings*, 37–38) reads 6:7–8 as an echo of agricultural metaphors in Philo regarding education and cultivating knowledge of virtue (especially in *de Agricultura* 9–18). The context of 5:11–14 would have invited an interpretation of Heb 6:7–8 in terms of Greco-Roman theory of education were it not for the intervention of 6:4–6, which moves the audience from the realm of education to the sphere of reciprocity and positions them, therefore, to hear 6:7–8 against *this* background rather than in the context of 5:11–14.

suggests, indeed, a noxious, hurtful return) should expect unfavorable treatment, even hostility and vengeance where favor once existed. Jewish scriptural texts provide some of the raw linguistic materials, but the social dynamics of reciprocity provide the argumentative frame.

Turning to the claim for which the argument from analogy seeks to provide confirmation, the relevant question concerns whether 6:4–6 indeed articulates a scenario involving patron-client roles and expectations. Interpreters often approach this passage by trying to answer questions like, "Is the author describing people who have been 'saved,' or who are merely semi-converts who have not yet experienced salvation?" Such a question is itself highly problematic, since the author of Hebrews does not use the language of salvation to speak of past acts of God or Christ on behalf of human beings, reserving the term to describe a deliverance coming at Christ's return or an inheritance about to be received in the future (1:14; 9:28).[21] On this basis alone, it is inappropriate to force theological categories of contemporary (Protestant) interest—are these people "saved" or "not yet saved"?—onto the text rather than allow the author to determine how we categorize the people to whom he refers in this hypothetical

21. Deliverance or salvation is something that the believers are "about to inherit" (1:14). It is this future deliverance (1:14) to which the phrase "such a great deliverance (2:3) specifically refers back. Deliverance is something that will be manifested when Christ comes "a second time" (9:28). It was what Noah attained at the end of his faithful response to God's command (11:7). The uses of the term in 2:10; 5:9; 6:9 lack any clear time frame, and so weigh neither in favor of *nor* against the general observation about when a believer is "delivered" ("saved") in Hebrews. The author of Hebrews is also not alone in viewing "salvation" as something lying ahead of the believer. 1 Peter (1:5, 9–10; 2:3) also retains a more thoroughly "eschatological" use of this concept.

argument (hypothetical, because the author himself affirms in 6:9 that it does not apply to the addressees themselves, at least not for the present).

The author presents this group of people as those who have received God's gifts, who have been benefitted by God's generosity. The author has put careful thought into the rhetorical crafting of 6:4–5. The hearers are struck by wave after wave of participial phrases, which together exhibit the rhetorical device of "accumulation," that give definition to an unspecified group of people, and it is specifically experiences of divine benefits that the preacher is piling up:

1. These people were "enlightened" (*phōtisthentas*), a common term in Christian culture for reception of the Christian gospel and its positive effects (See John 1:9; 1 Cor 4:5; 2 Cor 4:4–6; Eph 1:18; 2 Tim 1:10; 1 Pet 2:9; 2 Pet 1:10), implying a distinct advantage over those who remain "in the dark" about the requirements of God and the future of the world.

2. They have tasted God's "goodness," the combination of "being enlightened" and "tasting" that the Lord is good recalling LXX Ps 33:6, 8, a text promoting continued hope in God, fear of the Lord, and obedience to God through the assurance of enjoying God's protection and patronage (LXX Ps 33:4–7, 11).

3. They have received "the heavenly gift," the exact content of which is elusive, but which takes us even more directly into the social intertexture of patron-client scripts. The author's discussion of the ways in which the subjects of Heb 6:4–5 have been benefitted is setting up certain expectations concerning their response.

4. They have "become sharers of the Holy Spirit," which refers to one of the principal benefactions of God lavished
   upon the early church (see Gal 3:1–5; 4:1–7; 2 Cor 1:22;
   5:5; John 14:15–17; 16:13–15; Acts 10:44–48; 11:15–18).

5. They have "tasted the good word of God" (*kalon . . .
   rhēma*), a phrase possibly informed by Josh 21:45 and
   23:15, texts that speak of Israel hearing *ta rhēmata
   ta kala*, the "good words" of God, signifying God's
   promises.

6. These promises may, in turn, be specified by the next
   gift, the experience of the "powers" or "wonders" belonging and pointing to the "coming age," or the whole
   may look back upon their reception of the "good word"
   of the gospel and the divine confirmation that accompanied it (Heb 2:2–4).

The repetitive participial phrases present this unspecified
group of people as recipients of multiple, valuable, persistent
benefits from God. In terms of the social logic of the addressees' life-world, God's bountiful and persistent cultivation of
these recipients makes the response of a crop of gratitude
(honoring God, serving God, standing up for God's name) all
the more pressing—and amplifies the disgrace and injustice
of disrupting the dance of grace that God's generosity has
initiated.

The final participial phrase that rounds out the description of this group presents an unexpected outcome. Those
who have enjoyed these very great privileges, gifts, and promises—who have been granted every incentive and resource
to remain connected with the giver of such gifts—should
never "fall away" (6:6). And, as the larger context of the letter

shows, "falling away" here is not the result of some unavoidable misfortune: it is the product of a value judgment that sets more store in society's friendship than God's beneficence.[22] Enacting this value judgment, this conscious choice of friendship with the society and rejection of one's obligations toward God, is further described in terms of "crucifying afresh the Son of God to one's own disadvantage" and "holding him up to public humiliation."[23] Here we arrive at the information that provides the rationale for the impossibility of renewing such people to repentance. In their slight regard for God's gifts and promises, they have made the vicious response of offering insult to, even bringing disgrace upon, their benefactor. This was widely recognized as an unjust act meriting opprobrium, provoking the injured party to seek satisfaction and to exclude the offender from future favor.

Seneca wrote that an ingrate might not be punished by law, but he or she will certainly be punished by the public court of opinion and by his own awareness of being branded as ungrateful (*Ben.* 3.17.1–2). Dio Chrysostom, the orator and philosopher from Prusa, writes at length in his 31st oration about the disgrace of insulting one's benefactors when one ought to be taking the utmost care to continue to show them honor,

22. Both Hughes (*Hebrews*, 218 n.68) and Lane assert that the aorist tense of the participle "indicates a decisive moment of commitment to apostasy" (Lane, *Hebrews 1–8*, 142). This is problematic not only in the weight it puts on the significance of the aorist (the "undefined") tense (see Stagg, "Abused Aorist") but also in running counter to other images the author of Hebrews uses for the same action, many of which suggest not a "moment of decision" but a process of "drifting away" (2:1, for example; see also 3:13 for "hardening," and 4:1 and 12:15 for simply "falling short" for the goal, none of which suggest the "decisive moment").

23. Cf. H. Schlier, "Παραδειγματίζω," *TDNT* 2:32.

and not just as long as it is convenient and economical to do so. Those who honor benefactors "all people regard as worthy of favor" (*Or.* 31.7), but "those who insult their benefactors will by nobody be esteemed to deserve a favor" (31.65). Just as a person refuses to have dealings twice with a dishonest merchant, or to entrust a second deposit to someone who has lost the first one, so, Dio claims, the person who acts ungratefully should expect to be excluded from future favors (31.38, 65).

The addressees, themselves familiar with the reciprocal expectations and obligations of patrons and clients, will therefore understand and accept the "impossibility" advanced by the author. For them, it would not have been a question of the ingrate's *inability* to enter into a repentant frame of mind a second time or the ineffectiveness of further preaching.[24] The author excludes such speculation with the example of Esau, who deeply "repented" of his decision, but who was given no opportunity to return to his favored place no matter how sorry he was. After spurning God's gifts for the sake of temporal safety and approval, after breaking off the dance ungraciously, the ungrateful clients could not expect to be able to begin that journey to God's promised inheritances again. "Repentance" (*metanoia*) was the first building block in the author's description of the addressees' "foundation" in 6:1–3, the starting place of this journey where they went from being God's enemies to God's beneficiaries. That precious gift of a first repentance must itself be valued and preserved intact.[25]

24. This is implicit in Long, *Hebrews*, 73.

25. The author may conceive of repentance itself as a gift of God (so Lane, *Hebrews 1–8*, 142). For Philo, repentance is something that God can grant or withhold: "Many souls have desired to repent and not been permitted by God to do so" (*Leg.* 3.213; Attridge, *Hebrews*, 168 n. 25). Wisdom of Solomon also speaks of repentance as an opportunity allowed

In this context, the agricultural analogy functions to underscore for the hearers God's expectation of a fair return for the experience of God's benefits enumerated in Heb 6:4–5. The question facing the audience is, what kind of beneficiaries will they prove to be—base or honorable, ungrateful or reliable? Will they prove to be fruitful soil, and receive the greater gifts yet to come as fit recipients of God's ongoing favor, or will they prove to be bad soil, bringing forth an unpleasant and even hurtful response? To get the hearers thinking in such terms amounts to a major ideological victory for the author: he has transferred the decision about the relative merits and debits of remaining connected with the Christian group to a question about whether or not to respond nobly to God for all God's gifts, a question for which there is really only *one* answer. To the extent, then, that the hearers continue to regard the elements of their Christian experience as divine gifts, to that extent they will continue to invest themselves in and identify themselves with the Christian sect. Returning to the favor of society now explicitly carries the heavy price tag of alienating God through rank ingratitude toward God and God's Son.

The author goes on to affirm that the hearers have acted up to this point as noble recipients of God's gifts. They have

by God: the Canaanites were judged "little by little" to give them this "space for repentance" (*topon metanoias*, Wis 12:10; cf. Heb 12:16). God is known to block repentance until judgment is executed upon the sinners (Exod 7:3–4; 8:28; 10:1; 11:10; 1 Sam 2:25; Isa 6:9–10). Repentance is thus widely seen in Jewish culture as a gift, not a given: those who make ill use of the gift the first time can by no means count on a second opportunity to receive and use the gift. If the author of Hebrews shares this view, "repentance" would signify a welcome back into favor more than the internal experience of feeling guilty or the change of mind that "repentance" signifies for so many today (particularly in light of Esau's experience of great sorrow and regret without it effecting "repentance," Heb 12:16–17).

embodied the response in their own setting that the good soil does in the agricultural analogy, bringing forth good fruits for their fellow members within the group by investing themselves and their resources in one another. The author encourages them to persist in that which gives them this confidence, namely "the love which you show in God's name, serving the saints and continuing so to serve" (6:10). This concretizes the metaphorical language of 6:7–8, drawing out what the "real-life" counterparts to bearing suitable vegetation are. The hearers have already been producing "suitable vegetation" for those for whose sake they were being cultivated by means of God's gifts, namely for their Christian family. As they have made, and continue to make, a "just" return for God's benefits,[26] God will not be "unjust" to forget their nobility as clients and to continue to show them God's favor. The passage in this way serves another prominent goal of the sermon, namely shaping the kind of community that fosters sufficiently strong internal bonds and effectively marshals aid to withstand opposition from the more powerful social bodies outside the group (Heb 3:12–13; 10:24–25; 13:1–3, 16). Their service on behalf of one another becomes a source of assurance of God's ongoing favor, since they are responding appropriately to God's gifts bestowed thus far. Perseverance in such activity is linked with the outcome of "better things, the things having salvation" (cf. 1:14; 5:9),

26. On the specific idea that service rendered toward fellow believers is a service rendered to God (a response God will not "forget" but rather will reward), see Matt 25:31–46; Heb 13:16 (also Attridge, *Hebrews*, 175 n. 110). Heb 6:7–8 facilitates this understanding of how one responds correctly to God's gifts, for the benefit of rain is given to produce crops to benefit the eaters, not the rain giver. God's beneficence reaches out in this manner in widening ripples rather than returning to God's self.

such that mutual edification, support, and service emerges as the course that avoids the "fire" of 6:8 and preserves the enjoyment of God as Ally rather than Destroyer.[27]

Hebrews 6:1–12 thus contributes powerfully to the author's agenda for the hearers, namely motivating the congregation to press on to the end of the journey that began at their conversion, to press on in the direction that God's past gifts and promises of future benefactions lead them, to continue investing in the Christian group and in one another's perseverance unto perfection, and thus to continue to resist pressures from outside the group to re-assimilate to their old patterns of living and their former social networks. Hebrews 6:1 proposes this course of action as the natural consequence of the course of the journey begun by their conversion and traveled thus far. Hebrews 6:4–8 underscores the necessity of embracing this course of action, since to do otherwise would be to show rank ingratitude for the gifts God has already given, and thus to exchange the experience of God's ongoing favor for the experience of wrath at God's visitation. 6:9–12 affirms the hearers insofar as they have mirrored the good soil, making a good return on God's gifts by investing in one another, thus cementing their commitment to continuing in this course of action. The background of the social knowledge and practice of benefaction and reciprocity gives us access to the dynamics the hearers would have heard reflected throughout the passage, and to the presuppositions they bring to the text (e.g., regarding the behaviors of clients and patrons) as they participate in following its argumentation.

27. Craddock ("Hebrews," 76) looks to the effects and presentation of other "fires" in Hebrews (notably 10:27, but also 12:25–29), arguing cogently against the possibility that this burning seeks to restore or renew the soil. See also Lane, *Hebrews 1–8*, 143.

Legitimating Commitment to the Sect as a Summons to Show Gratitude to God

From a close investigation of a single passage, we turn to take a bird's eye overview of the whole of Hebrews, intended to show how the social background of patronage, friendship, and reciprocity informs and holds together a great deal of this sermon. This particular background illumines how the various segments and threads of the sermon relate to one another as they come together to form a coherent argument as the basis for a call to persevere in gratitude, and thus to remain committed to the social body formed around, and distinguished from outsiders by, the same experience of divine favor.

The sermon has long been recognized to consist of alternating sections of "exposition" (or sustained discussion of a particular theme) and "exhortation" (sustained recommendations concerning appropriate behavior to adopt in light of the points established in the "expositions").[28] Comparison is the outstanding feature of the "expository" sections of Hebrews. The preacher holds up the "Son" next to various other figures from the sacred cosmos and history of Israel, in each case demonstrating the Son's superiority. Thus, the Son is greater than the angels (1:5–14); the Son is greater than Moses (3:1–6); and, in greatest detail, the Son is a better-placed and more effective mediator than the Levitical Priests (7:1—10:18). It is significant that angels, Moses, and the Levitical Priests were all *mediator* figures in the Jewish tradition inherited by the Christian movement. Angels brought the prayers of people before God and were involved in delivering answers (see, for example, Tob 3:16–17; 12:12–15; *T. Levi* 3:4–7). They were

28. Büchsel, "Hebräerbrief"; Gyllenberg, "Composition."

also mediators of the Old Covenant, it being commonly believed in the first century that angels delivered God's Law to Moses (see Gal 3:19; Acts 7:38, 53; *Jub.* 1:27–29; 2:1). Moses was also involved in the mediation of the first covenant, but he also interceded on behalf of the people (Exod 32:7–14, 30–34; Num 14:17–20; *T. Mos.* 11.17), and was believed to have a continuing role in intercession (Pseudo-Philo, *LAB* 19.11). The Levitical priests, of course, were chiefly responsible for repairing the relationship between people and God by means of the sacrificial cult day-by-day, year-by-year, and thus securing God's ongoing favor.

To what use does the author put his demonstration that the Son is greater than angels (1:5–14)? He calls the hearers to give the deliverance (the "salvation," *sōtēria*) that the Son announced and made possible—a benefit of extreme value—its due weight. And if the message announced through angels was so weighty that transgression meant execution, the hearers needed to respect and pay attention to the message announced through the Son, who possessed greater dignity than angels, all the more (2:1–4). The preacher goes on to explain how the Son has used his exalted status to benefit the hearers in many ways, pioneering the way to glory for all the sons and daughters God was bringing into his household (2:9–10), breaking the power of the fear of death over their lives (2:14–15), and "helping" the hearers, having been prepared by his own endurance of suffering and trial to offer help with the utmost sympathy and dedication (2:16–18).

The point of the preacher's comparison of the Son with Moses is to point out that, while Moses was indeed faithful, it was only as a servant *in* God's house, but the Son is faithful *over* God's house (3:1–6). Because Jesus is God's Son, he is a better placed mediator within the household of the Father God, just as those seeking the emperor's favor through the mediation of a member of his close family would enjoy greater assurance of the success of their suit than those approaching him through a servant or lower-level administrator.[29]

The fact that the heart of Hebrews speaks in the idiom of priesthood, sacrificial ritual, and sacred spaces (5:1–10; 7:1—10:18) should not obscure the fact that the discussion is still entirely focused on the benefits Jesus has brought the hearers, establishing a grace-relationship between God and human beings, and on the cost to himself of his mediation. What is at stake is access to God's favor and benefits. These chapters on Christ's priesthood and sacrifice explore the "mechanics" of his mediation, how he became qualified to serve as the ultimate bridge-builder between God and people, and how he brought the hearers to their unprecedented place in God's favor, cleansing and consecrating them to move across the threshold into the heavenly Holy of Holies. By comparing the Son with the Levitical priests,[30] the preacher hopes to imprint

29. De Ste. Croix ("Suffragium," 41) notes that the members of a great person's extended household could serve as brokers of that person's favor. The list includes "his friends, who had the ear of the great man; their friends, even, at only one further remove; even the personal slaves of the great man, who often, for the humble client, could procure or withhold audience with the patron—all these satellites shone with various degrees of reflected glory and were well worth courting." Clearly, those "satellites" closest to the star at the center shone with the brightest reflected glory. According to Richard Saller (*Patronage*, 59), the close relatives of the emperor, especially his sons, were sought after as mediators of the emperor's favor: their close, familial relationship to the patron gave great hope of success (see, for example the letter of Fronto, *Ad M. Caes.* 5.34, 37).

30. The author's choice of the Levitical priesthood as the object of comparison is dictated not by the presumed situation of the hearers

on his hearers the value of having the Son as their personal patron, mediating their access to God and maintaining God's favorable reception of the believers as the Son's own clients. God himself affirmed Jesus' mediation with an oath, something that did not undergird the Levitical priests' mediation. Jesus has no need to offer sacrifices for his own sins before being able to approach God on behalf of his clients. Jesus stands in closer proximity to God, in the real sanctuary in heaven itself rather than its copy in Jerusalem. Jesus offered a more effective sacrifice—not animal sacrifices that deal only with external defilements, but a perfect act of obedience that suffices to remove sin from the consciences of his people *and* from the sight of God. He bound God and people together under a better covenant, the one promised in Jeremiah 31, a covenant that fits human beings to enter God's presence in the abiding realm through the decisive removal of the defilements of sin.

The Son continues to use his exalted position at the right hand of the throne of God to provide the hearers with ongoing access to God's help, whatever challenges they might be facing, so that they don't ever need to give up or fall short of God's good goal for them:

> Therefore, since we have a great high priest who has passed through the heavens, Jesus, the Son of God, let us hold onto what we profess. For we don't have a high priest who is unable to empathize with our weaknesses, but one who has been tested in every way that we are, yet without sin. So let us draw near

returning to a dependence upon the temple cult (and thus reassimilating to non-Christian Judaism), but by the fact that they are the only other mediators of the favor of the One God. Comparing Jesus to the priests of Greco-Roman cults would be meaningless, as the latter stand in relation to no "true" gods at all.

with boldness to the throne of favor, in order that
we may receive mercy and find favor for timely
help. (Heb 4:14–16)

The Son's presence there at God's right hand, in the heavenly
Holy of Holies, becomes the anchor for the hearers' hope that
they, too, will indeed arrive in the eternal Promised Land that
God has prepared for them (6:19–20). Jesus stands ready to
make sure the believers receive whatever timely help they
need as they run their course following their pioneer, so that
they may all arrive securely in the eternal homeland.

The author declares that the first half of his sermon has a
single main point: "we have such a great high priest," we have
such a well-placed, effective, tireless mediator of divine favor
(8:1–2)! He calls the hearers throughout the sermon, then, to
respond appropriately to the Son. The most exalted figure in
the cosmos besides God lowered himself in the incarnation,
embraced rejection and hostility, and died a shameful death
to bring the hearers such great benefits for this life and the life
beyond this visible realm. He paid the highest cost to bring
the greatest goods to his own, and to connect them securely
to God's favor and God's promise of an abiding homeland in
God's presence. How, then, should the hearers respond?

The author urges them to give this gift of deliverance the
attention it deserves—and the attention and weight that the
Son's honor commands (2:1–4). He urges them to keep their
hearts fixed on the benefits Christ has brought, and to make
full use of them. If the Son offers access to "mercy and favor
for timely help," the hearers need to "draw near to the throne
of favor" in prayer, intercession, and worship together to take
full advantage of the access the Son has opened up at such
cost to himself (4:14–16). If the Son has cleansed them for

entrance into the heavenly Holy Places at the cost of his own death and the spilling of his own blood for them, the hearers need once again to "draw near with a sincere heart in full confidence" (10:22), valuing and making full use of what the Son has provided, rather than turning away from the destiny that Jesus has opened up for them in order to seek instead the friendship and favor of their neighbors once again.

They need to maintain their enviable status as "partners" with the exalted Lord and part of the household of God over which the Son presides by maintaining their hope, their boldness, and their pride in the honor the Son has conferred upon them (3:6, 14). The author urges them to invest themselves fully in attaining the promises God holds out before them (4:11). And they need to help one another keep their minds fixed on the gifts and the promises that have come to them from God through Christ, so as to help their fellow clients keep responding to God and God's Son appropriately (3:12–13; 4:1; 10:24–25; 12:15–17), no longer holding back from fulfilling their responsibilities to one another in God's household (5:11–14).

In sum, "since we are in the process of receiving an unshakable kingdom," the preacher urges the hearers, "let us show gratitude" (12:28). In addition to showing their appreciation for God's gifts by keeping them ever foremost in their minds, making full use of them, and fixing their hearts on the good things promised and yet to come, this gratitude involves bringing honor to God and to Christ through public testimony—holding onto "the profession of our hope without wavering" (10:23) and offering "the fruit of lips that profess God's name" (13:15); through loyalty—associating with Christ and fellow Christians, even when costly (10:24–25, 32–34;

13:3); and through acts of service. As those whom God has cultivated through his many benefactions, the hearers are to bear the kind of fruit God looks for—acts of love, kindness, and support for their fellow believers, pouring themselves out to sustain their sisters and brothers in their time of need (6:9–10; 10:32–34; 13:1–3, 16).

Thus far, we have looked largely at the positive incentives offered by the author in terms of naming, evaluating, and responding to the benefits that the community has experienced and will yet experience. There is another side to the author's strategy, a stick that corresponds to the carrot, as it were—and this stick is given its power also from the social logic of reciprocity that we have been examining. The person who withdraws from the Christian group in response to the social pressure of shaming and other deviancy-control measures, who thus denies association with the name of Jesus, makes a statement about Jesus' patronage and the value of the gifts that the person has experienced as a result of Jesus' mediation of divine favor. That statement is, simply, that these gifts are not worth what it has cost to keep them, and that the patron-client relationship forged with God through the Son is less valuable that the patron-client and friendship relationships that the person has lost within the larger social body. The insult, the affront, in such withdrawal, then, would be obvious to the audience, as would, then, the danger and disadvantage of making an enemy out of so powerful (and hitherto *good*) a benefactor.

Hebrews 6:4–8 was an important example of how the "stick" works in this sermon, but it is only one of several powerful and relevant warning passages. In 3:7–4:11, the author holds up the exodus generation, the Hebrews who left Egypt with Moses, as an admonitory example of the dangers of showing a lack of trust (*pistis*) in the Divine Patron and his promises. He focuses on the episode recounted in Numbers 14. The Hebrews stand on the threshold of the Promised Land, and disobey God's command to move in and take possession because their spies have brought back a report that makes them fear the strength of the people living in that land. "Distrust" (*apistia*) is the core issue here (3:12, 19). The Hebrews had God's promise that he would give them the land of Canaan; they had the experience of God's many acts of deliverance and help all along their journey from Egypt to this point (emphasized in Psalm 95:9, recited in Heb 3:9), which should have put their Patron's reliability beyond all question. Fearing the indigenous peoples, however, they entertain doubts about God's ability to fulfill those promises and begin to make plans to return to the relative safety of Egypt, even though it meant a return to the slavery from which God took pains to liberate them. Their response provokes God to wrath against those whom God had desired to benefit, but who had been disobedient, trampled the promise, and faltered in their trust.[31] The result was the irrevocable loss of access to the promised benefit: "As I swore in my wrath, 'They shall not enter my rest'" (Heb 3:11, 18; 4:3). Failure to trust and to obey the Patron resulted in exclusion from future benefactions—a warning that the author goes on to apply directly to his hearers' situation (4:1, 11).

Another important and striking warning passage is found in 10:26–31, which is offered specifically as an incen-

31. The author of Numbers had already explicitly equated the Hebrews' lack of trust with an affront to God's honor that would provoke God (Num 14:11). On Heb 3:7—4:11, see further deSilva, *Perseverance*, 140–69.

tive to the audience to hold onto the hope that they professed, not withdrawing from assembling in public with other believers, but rather encouraging one another to persevere in gratitude and supporting one another in that perseverance with acts of love (10:23–25):

> If we voluntarily continue to sin after receiving the knowledge of the truth, no sacrifice for sins is left, but only a frightful anticipation of judgment and of a fire eager to consume the adversaries. Anyone who transgresses Moses' law dies without mercy on the word of two or three witnesses. Of how much worse punishment, do you think, will the one who has trampled the Son of God underfoot, who has treated the blood of the covenant by which he or she was sanctified as ordinary, and who has insulted the Spirit of favor be judged worthy? For we know the one who said, "Vengeance belongs to me; I will repay." And again, "The Lord will judge his people." It is a frightful thing to fall into the hands of the living God. (Heb 10:26–31)

The first hearers were under considerable centrifugal pressures to shrink away from the Christian group, to "draw back" from God and one another, as they reversed their direction and went back to the bosom of the larger society. But tempering one's response to God out of concern for the response of one's neighbors and society, the author claims, constitutes a deliberate affront to God that leads to encountering God as Judge rather than as Patron. Seeking the approval of sinners (the "unconverted" outside the group, who reject the message and the Messiah it announced) rather than being willing to shoulder the cost of belonging to the company of the redeemed, moreover, acts out a response of ingratitude of the basest sort. A person who acts in this manner tells God, in effect, that God's gifts, provided only at such cost to God's Son, are not worth what they cost to keep in terms of the temporary deprivations and the "hostility of sinners" that have to be endured. The promise is not worth the perseverance.

In this warning passage, the preacher claims that such a response amounts to a gross insult to the Son and a gross undervaluing of his gifts. It responds to his favor with insult and affront, a strikingly inappropriate, even unthinkable, return for favor. It is the equivalent of trampling him underfoot in the public arena. But the Son is the One whose dignity is such that he sits at God's right hand and awaits his enemies being put down under his own feet (1:13; 8:1; 10:12–13)! What will be the fate of those who have failed to honor the Son as he merits, let alone those who throw his gifts back in his face?! Such a person becomes the target of God's satisfaction of the Son's slighted honor, a fearsome prospect indeed. On the one hand—the hand that holds the carrot—we saw how Jesus' remarkable proximity to God (genealogically, as "Son," and spatially, as one who stands in God's real presence in the divine realm) makes him the most effective person to connect people to God—more effective than all other mediators known in the history of Jewish tradition (e.g., angels, Moses, and the Levitical priests). On the other hand, the author's depiction of Jesus' exalted honor magnifies also the danger of abusing Jesus' honor through any course of action that suggested disloyalty or a de-valuing of one's connection with Jesus (like apostasy, whether overt or gradual and quiet). As the author has painted the audience's situation, while there is limitless advantage in continuing to own connection with Jesus and to respond to him with loyalty and gratitude, no matter what the cost in this world, there is significant danger in denying or minimizing one's connection with Jesus.

In light of the dangers of failing to make an appropriate response to the favor of God in Christ, the author urges the hearers to remember their obligation of gratitude, and to respond honorably to one who has lavished such costly gifts and such promises of future benefaction so generously and graciously upon them. If they will keep their "boldness" (*parrhēsia*, 10:35) vis-à-vis their neighbors and the larger society that brings its pressures to bear upon them, if they continue witnessing through word and deed to their Patron, the value of his gifts and promises, and the solidarity of believers, they will keep enjoying their "boldness" (*parrhēsia*, 10:19; cf. 4:16) vis-à-vis God. In particular, he encourages them to be willing to pay the costs of being associated with God and God's Christ, of being associated with the people of God and God's promise, in this life. He holds up "trust" (*pistis*, "faith") as a cardinal virtue to display in their situation—trust that "God exists and rewards those who earnestly seek him" (11:6). And the trust that remains in God's favor and attains God's promises often requires moving out of the places of status and into the margins of one's society (11:1—12:3). He urges them to endure "the hostility of sinners" courageously like wrestlers in the arena or like youths being shaped by rigorous exercises for a bright future in a better government (12:1–11), bearing Christ's reproach, which he first bore for them, mindful of the fact that they have not yet come near making a full return to him for the life he poured out for them (12:4).

In light of all this, the closing verse is much more than a pious wish, a liturgical addendum. It is the preacher's heartfelt desire that, indeed, "grace" (*charis*) will be with all of them.

He has held before them the multifaceted grace that God has lavished upon them and that the Son has secured for them. He has spurred them on by exhortation and warning to return grace for grace, to walk in gratitude for the gifts they have received and are yet promised. In this way, God's grace will have its full effect in and among them—not in their receiving it merely, but in their using God's gifts, in their allowing of God's grace fully to shape their response to one another and their witness in their setting, and in their fixing of their hearts more securely on the graces yet to be enjoyed when Christ comes a second time, not to deal with sin, but to deliver those who are eagerly waiting for him (9:28). In all these ways, the author seeks to confirm their hearts—to make them firm and securely fixed—in "grace" (13:9).

Conclusion

The author of Hebrews has drawn extensively on shared knowledge about a broad-based social institution, its roles, and its "rules" in order to shape the hearers' thinking about what is at stake in their situation and what scripts ought to shape their response within that situation. While, on the one hand, he addresses their experience of the social pressures of shame and marginalization (see chapter three), he also introduces the scripts of noble clients and dishonorable clients into the audience's assessment of their situation and of their potential responses within that situation. These function as an effective rhetorical constraint upon the audience, moving them toward identifying ongoing commitment to the sect with responding appropriately and honorably to the God whose favor and gifts they have enjoyed since crossing over into the sect.

The author's warning that, for those who show such disregard for God's gifts as choose the friendship of society over the friendship of God, there is no return to favor serves an important social function. He draws a sharp line in the sand at the boundary between the sect and the society and declares, "if you cross this line, there's no coming back," legitimating this claim in the fundamental logic of the social institutions of patronage and friendship. The social effects of the author's discourse is to focus the audience on that boundary, to make the line between sect and society clearer and more significant, and to make them ask themselves and each other which side of the line each person really wants to be on. He does this in the context of the sacred knowledge shared by the group, which cumulatively serves to highlight the importance of being found "inside" the sect, where God is experienced as generous patron, rather than "outside" amongst those who continue to act as God's enemies, who will encounter God as a consuming fire (10:27–28; 12:29). The author's discourse is calculated to make the audience afraid (quite literally *afraid*; 4:1; 10:27, 31) to cross back over that boundary, and thus to motivate them to draw away from that boundary and closer together at the center of the sect. It is this same social "movement" that the author positively encourages throughout the sermon, calling the audience to "draw near to the throne of favor" and, at the same time, to draw and remain near to the threshold between this realm and the divine realm (4:16; 10:22; 12:22) and, in so doing, to remain on the "inside" of the line between sect and society.

FIVE

Sociorhetorical Strategy III: Reinforcing Group Identity and Commitment

DEFINING THE COURT OF REPUTATION

A particular group will use both honor and shame as means to enforce conformity within that group to the values and behaviors promoted by the group. In a complex society, however, different groups use honor and shaming to motivate adherence to each particular group's values and ideals. What is valued (and, thus, honored) by one group may in fact be censured by a different group. It is very important, therefore, that a member of one group learn whose opinion in regard to honor and dishonor to value, and whose opinion about the same to exclude from consideration, or at least to accord secondary status. In other words, it makes a great deal of difference who constitutes a person's "court of reputation" or "court of opinion." To the extent that this court of opinion is limited to other members of the same social subgroup, a person's sensitivity to honor and shame will result in reinforcing that person's commitment to the practices and ideals that the group values. In an earlier chapter we explored the strategies used by the author of Hebrews to insulate his audience from concern for the opinion of non-Christian groups. This is the "deconstructionist" aspect of the strategy of many minority cultures in the ancient Mediterranean. The positive counterpart is the establishment of an alternate court of opinion—the designation of a body of "significant others" before whom one is to feel shame, and whose approval and esteem one is to seek.

A minority group often offsets the minority status of its standards and opinion by including some supra-social entity like God or Nature within this body of significant others. The opinion of one's fellow group members is thus anchored in, and legitimated by, a higher court of reputation, whose judgments are of greater importance and more lasting consequence than the opinion of the disapproving (but merely human) majority or dominant culture.[1] The opinion and evaluation of the majority is unreliable precisely because the majority is not devoted to this higher Judge and the standards of that court.[2] It is not surprising, therefore, to find God and Christ at the center of the court of opinion to which the author of Hebrews (like the authors of most early Christian

1. Philosophers frequently appeal to a higher court for validation of their ideals (see, e.g., Plato, *Gorgias* 526D–527D; Epictetus, *Diss.* 1.30.1), as do Jewish authors, who appeal to God's approval and the hope of honor in God's presence to uphold strict adherence to Torah in the face of pressure from the dominant culture to assimilate (e.g., Sir 23:18–19; *4 Macc* 17:4–5).

2. Cf. Epictetus, *Diss.* 4.5.22; Plato, *Cri.* 44C; Seneca, *Constant.* 13.2, 5; Isa 51:7–8; Wis 2:1–24; 5:4–6.

literature) draws attention, refocusing the individual's desire on attaining God's approval and esteem.

The conviction that one's behavior was honorable in God's sight could be enough to offset the disapproval and rejection of society. For the author of Hebrews, God's vindication of Jesus manifests both the radical difference between God's evaluation and the world's and the ability of God's verdict to overturn the verdict of the lower, human court. Where the unbelieving society condemned Jesus to the most severe humiliation (12:2), God has granted him the place of greatest honor. Because God has the last word on a person's honor, the divine court of opinion is elevated above any human court that opposes God's standards and criteria of evaluation.

The author frequently calls the audience to give thought to God's evaluation of them, warning them to show the greatest concern for God's opinion. A passage that is frequently read as a text about the power of Scripture actually speaks more directly about God as Judge of the totality of human life:

> God's word is alive and full of power, sharper than any double-edged sword, cutting through to the point of separating soul from spirit, joint from marrow, discerning the heart's musings and intentions. No creature can remain hidden before him, but all are naked, with their throats exposed, before the eyes of him to whom we have to give account. (4:12–13)

The author admonishes his audience to have a care that the whole of their lives be carried on with a view to God's approval, for indeed all of life is subject to God's inquiry and will be evaluated not by the standards approved by society, but by

God.[3] The author also closes his oration by pointing the addressees to God's approval: "May the God of peace . . . make you firm in every good thing in order that you may do his will; may he work in us that which pleases him, through Jesus Christ" (13:20–21). The goal of the believer's life, therefore, is to please God, that is, to live by God's standards of honorable behavior and so gain God's approval and testimony, which count above all others' esteem.[4] The author assures the addressees that God remembers their acts of love and service, signaling approval and the prospect of future reward (6:10). In the same way, the erasure of sins from God's memory assures the believers that their honor in God's sight will be untarnished (10:17). The believer may stand before God's court of reputation with confidence, knowing that God's recollection of his or her noble deeds (as defined by the Christian minority culture) will guarantee eternal honor (overturning the disgrace currently imposed upon them by outsiders).

The strongest expression of God as the "significant other" most to be concerned about appears in the references to the last judgment, when the divine evaluation of all people will be made manifest. In light of the coming "Day," that is, the day of judgment, the author urges his hearers to encourage one another in doing the noble deeds that will result in honor before that court, which has the final word on a person's honor or dishonor: "Let us consider one another unto an outburst of love and good works, not abandoning your gatherings, as is the habit of some, but encouraging one another, and all the

3. The openness of all parts of a person's life to divine scrutiny is familiar from the Jewish tradition (as in Ps 139 or Sir 23:18–19), but also from Greco-Roman philosophical texts (see Epictetus, *Diss.* 2.8.13–14).

4. Cf. 2 Cor 5:9–10; Epictetus, *Diss.* 1.30.1.

more as you see the Day drawing closer" (10:24–25). On that day, the visible realm will be removed and the invisible world disclosed (12:26–27): thus the people of faith who have evaluated and acted with the invisible world in view (11:3, 7, 27) will be vindicated. Those who have remained loyal to their Patron will receive the promised reward and salvation (9:28), while those who have enacted ingratitude through apostasy, or have otherwise transgressed God's values, will receive lasting disgrace (cf. 10:29–31). Fear of God's censure rightly outweighs fear of society's censure, thus elevating continued commitment to the group's values and valued practices.[5]

The community of believers constitutes the visible body of significant others who reinforce the worth and honor of one another according to the values and standards projected onto the heavenly court (or, in less sociological and more religious terms, revealed by God in the message announced in the Son). The community praises and censures its members using the deep-seated desire for honor and aversion toward shame to nurture internalization of the community's ideals and valued practices. As long as the interaction between group members remains frequent and vibrant, its members will seek approval primarily in the community's estimation. The author's hortatory thrust pushes strongly in the direction of the maintenance of this alternate court of reputation, seeking to strengthen the social base of support for the Christian worldview and for the practices and investments that are based upon that worldview.

---

5. For the use of the divine court among Greco-Roman philosophers and Jewish authors, Plato, *Gorg.* 526D–527A, and 2 Macc 6:26 provide fairly typical examples.

Sociologist Peter Berger calls this social base a "plausibility structure," a group of real-life people whose commitment to a particular worldview continues to hold that worldview up as "real" and "given" (hence, a "plausible" representation of reality) for each individual person within the group, and thus reinforces the commitment of any individual person to that worldview and the way of life built upon it.[6] The addressees of Hebrews live in an environment of wildly competing definitions of reality. A more imposing social body continues to reflect the "reality" of its own worldview (the worldview in which the Greco-Roman pantheon rules the cosmos, in which acts of piety and gratitude are properly directed toward them and toward the emperor, the vessel of divine favor) and impose this reflection of reality upon the members of the Christian community. Similarly, the local Jewish community seeks to re-establish its worldview (based on Torah observance as the proper response to the One God, the clear delineation of the lines around the "chosen" group in terms of such observance, and the like) as "real" in the minds of its wayward members who are now found among the Christian community. There are thus many challenges to the "givenness" or the "reality" of the Christian definitions of "the way the world really is" in God's sight," and, being a minority group, Christians have to work a whole lot harder to maintain the conviction that their view of reality is ultimately the right one, the one on the basis of which to make decisions about proper action and investment.

The author recognizes the important role that the community has to play in empowering the perseverance of the individual. The author expresses concern for the waning

6. Berger, *Sacred Canopy*, 45–47; see also Filson, *Yesterday*, 69.

commitment of some who are "abandoning the practice of meeting together" with the Christian assembly (10:25). The community has, to some extent, failed these individuals by not providing the level of group interaction and the reinforcement of group values that are essential for keeping members from looking again to the unbelieving society for the affirmation of their self-worth, and thus for preventing their returning to their former social networks and to the behaviors and ideals valued by the dominant Greco-Roman culture. The remaining believers' failure to become "teachers" by this point (5:11–14) is a failure to take an active role in helping their sisters and brothers to maintain their commitment to the worldview of the Christian group and to the behaviors that arise therefrom. These withdrawing individuals, on the other hand, have also failed their fellow Christians. The departure of some disciples is a diminishment of the whole, a negative, corrosive influence on the commitment of those who remain behind ("if they no longer find this Christian enterprise compelling, why exactly do we?"), and a loss of those human resources from the pool on which the whole community depends. The author is thus concerned to keep the remaining members moving in the direction of "drawing near" to one another, assuring them that this same motion means "drawing near" to God and to their heavenly inheritance (4:14–16; 10:22–25; 12:22–23).

The author directs the community members to remind one another of what constitutes valued and praiseworthy behavior, and to spur one another on to act nobly in the eyes of the group. Throughout his sermon, the author directs the audience to invest in reinforcing one another's commitment, and particularly to pay attention to one another, watching out for any signs that any particular individuals are beginning to succumb to the pressures and "anti-witness" of the society, and are thus moving away from commitment to the group and its ideals:

> Keep on the lookout, brothers and sisters, in case there be in any one of you a wicked, distrustful heart, inclined to turn away from the living God. But keep speaking encouragement to each other every day, as long as it is called "today," in order that no one of you become hardened by sin's deceitfulness. (3:12–13)

> Let us be afraid, then, lest, while there remains a promise of entering his rest, any one of you thinks it best to stop short. (4:1)

> Keep watching out lest any one of you fall short of God's gift, lest any "root of bitterness sprout up" and through it many become defiled, lest any one become carnal and godless like Esau, who sold his rights as the firstborn for the sake of a single meal. (12:15–16)

The community is given collective responsibility for reinforcing the loyalty and commitment of each member, praising those who enact the group's values and assuring the wavering. As the addressees take up the watchful stance and diligent intervention urged by the author, each member of the Christian community will experience the circle of believers more and more fully as, indeed, his or her significant others, whose opinion is paramount. The author himself forms an active part of this alternate court of opinion, censuring the addressees for their waning fervor and lack of zeal (5:11–14) and praising them for their displays of love and service (6:9–10) and for their former demonstration of commitment even at great cost (10:32–34). The community leaders (13:17) will also function as an important part of this alternate court, ascribing honor to the obedient and committed, rebuking the half-hearted.

The apparently unrelated exhortations of chapter 13 in fact continue to promote the author's goal of maintaining the strength of the plausibility structure. He urges that they continue to maintain "the love of a brother or a sister" (*philadelphia*, 13:1) for one another, taking on toward one another the responsibility of family. Only by making this level of investment in one another will the group be able to sustain the commitment of individual believers in obedience to the call of God that led them in directions contrary to the ways embraced by their other (former) social networks and society at large. Where members of the community regard (and treat) fellow believers as their closest family, moreover, the Christian group will also be the primary source of their identity and honor, as well as the primary group to whom they will owe their first duty and allegiance. The exhortation to provide hospitality for traveling fellow believers (13:2) links the local Christian community to the broader Christian minority culture, reminding the local community that it is not alone and, perhaps, not such a minority in the world after all. The author urges each community member to allow the plight of a fellow believer who has been targeted by the dominant social group as a "deviant" to touch him or her on the basis of their common bond, and to help such a person rather than turn a blind eye or stand off at a safe distance (13:3). Only the group that is willing to support its members under such conditions can maintain the loyalty and trust of its adherents, and show that society's court is not, after all, the final adjudicator of worth. The religious acts of "sacrifice" offered by the new congregation of the sanctified and accepted by God consist of praise and bold testimony (13:15), but also acts of kindness toward and sharing possessions especially with fellow Christians (13:16).

The alternate court of reputation is further broadened to include the historic community of faith, quite visibly in the "encircling cloud of witnesses" (12:1) made up of the past exemplars of faith, who now watch and judge the audience's performance in their own "contest."[7] While the visible community may be small, and its evaluation of the individual perhaps insignificant when compared to the esteem of the dominant majority, the invisible community that evaluates and ascribes honor by the same standards is overwhelming, spanning generations and transcending the earthly realm:

> You have drawn near to Mount Zion and to the city of the living God, Heavenly Jerusalem, and to myriads of angels joining in a festal song, and to the assembly of the first-born whose names are registered in the heavens, and to God, the judge of all, and to the spirits of the righteous who have been perfected, and to Jesus, the broker of a new covenant, and to the sprinkled blood that speaks a better word than did Abel's blood. (12:22–24)

Before *this* expansive court the believer is called to seek everlasting prestige. While the author seeks to neutralize any

7. Compare the use of this "invisible court of reputation" in *4 Macc* 13:17, where the seven brothers disregard the disgrace before the human court in the hope that "Abraham, Isaac, and Jacob will welcome us, and all the fathers will praise us."

sense of shame the addressees may have in the sight of unbe-lievers—that is, to urge them to regard as nothing the evalu-ation of outsiders, and hence to live free of the pressures to conform to the expectations and values of non-Christians—he also seeks to strengthen their sense of shame before one another (before the alternate "court of reputation"), so that their desire for honor may be fulfilled specifically through their Christian witness and commitments.

COMMITMENT MECHANISMS

Rosabeth Kanter developed a theory of commitment within religious groups and of the social mechanisms that nurture commitment. Kanter defines commitment as alignment be-tween the needs of the individual with actions or attitudes that maintain the group.[8] As the individual seeks his or her own fulfillment in some fundamental sense, he or she acts in a way that also ultimately serves the greater interests of the group. The presenting issue in the situation addressed by the author of Hebrews can be formulated as, essentially, a crisis of commitment. Some members of the group are beginning to act as if their own best interests are not those of the group, but rather as if being a fervent member of the group works against the individual's interests. For example, it is in the best interests of the group as a whole that its members meet to-gether regularly to confirm the group's identity and mobilize to pursue its mission, but some individuals have begun to consider their own interests to be jeopardized by continued identification with this group, and so have stopped associat-ing with it (10:24–25).

8. Kanter, *Commitment*, 66.

Kanter recognizes multiple dimensions at work in nurturing commitment. A person's commitment increases or wavers in relation to "the rewards and costs that are involved in participating in the system," his or her "emotional attachment to the people in the system," and the degree to which he or she finds "the norms and beliefs of the system" to be compelling.[9] A representative of the group seeking to strengthen commitment will need to "set in motion processes that reduce the value of other possible commitments and increase the value of commitment" to his or her particular group.[10] The author of Hebrews attends precisely to this task. We have already explored several strategies pursued by the author that contribute to fostering commitment in terms of each of the three dimensions noted above. The author renders the sect's "norms and beliefs" more compelling by reminding the audience of their experience of the divine, and specifically of the divine-human relationship, as a relationship of "grace" (thus requiring an array of responses that collectively enact "commitment"). In the same vein, the author rearticulates the "rewards and costs" of persevering as opposed to slackening commitment from within the framework of that divine-human relationship, demonstrating the exorbitant costs that follow upon failing commitment. The way the author has addressed the audience's experience of social shaming also contributes to the recalculation of rewards and costs by minimizing the cost of the loss of esteem in the eyes of outsiders to the group and by maximizing the rewards of steadfast endurance of the same (e.g., as divine discipline or as a contest in which everlasting repute is to be won). Finally, the author's

9. Ibid., 68.
10. Ibid., 72.

discourse is likely to enhance "emotional attachment to the people in the system" among the audience, recalling the ways in which they have pulled together in times of duress (6:9–10; 10:32–34) and stimulating the kind of supportive interaction that will bind group members more closely together.

The author's discourse can also be seen to nurture several of the processes that Kanter has identified as tending to increase commitment to a group. These processes are sacrifice, investment, renunciation, communion, mortification, and transcendence. Kanter's model proves a helpful inventory for investigating the sociorhetorical strategy of the author of Hebrews from a different angle.

Sacrifice and Investment

According to Kanter, "the process of sacrifice asks members to give up something as the price of membership."[11] This fosters commitment insofar as membership has now "cost" something and, thus, will be valued accordingly. The audience of Hebrews was, no doubt, required to give up certain practices and indulgences as a prerequisite to joining the Christian group—those practices to which the author now refers as "dead works" (6:1; 9:14)—but he does not dwell on this nor call for new "sacrifices" per se. Rather, he seems to focus more on the addressees' investment, the process by means of which group members "gain a stake in the group, commit current and future profits to it, so that [they] must continue to participate if [they are] going to realize those profits."[12] The author emphasizes how much the audience has invested themselves in the group and in one another up to this point,

11. Ibid., 76.
12. Ibid., 72.

reminding them of their investment of "work and the love [they] showed to the saints and continue to show" (6:10), as well as their earlier investment as they endured shame, persecution, and confiscation of physical property in the service of one another and for the sake of God (10:32–34). The author emphasizes the proximity of the return on the addressees' investment, the reward that the addressees have already all but secured, if only they remain committed for yet a short while (10:37): "Don't throw away your boldness, then, which holds a great reward in store; for you need endurance, so that, having done God's will, you may receive what was promised" (10:35–36). Kanter's definition of "investment" is all but a paraphrase of Heb 10:32–36.

The author is especially sensitive to the believers who have lost their property. His frequent use of vocabulary from the word group related to "inheritance" would hold special significance for them. They may have lost property (their earthly inheritance?) here on account of their casting in their lot with the Christian group, but they have become heirs of "better and lasting possessions" in a "heavenly homeland" that cannot be shaken (10:24; 11:16; 12:28). But, again, they "must continue to participate if [they are] going to realize those profits" (see 6:12; 9:15). Their faith itself—one might say their "commitment," their "firmness" in regard to their place in the new community and in the grace relationship with God—is the "title deed" or "guarantee" (11:1) of their future possession of this "better and lasting property."[13] The author calls for continued investment of resources in one an-

13. See Worley, "God's Faithfulness," 90–91 on the use of *hypostasis* (11:1) and *komizomai* (10:36) in commercial documents.

other (13:3, 16), as well as personal involvement in the lives and perseverance of fellow believers (3:13; 10:24; 12:15).

Renunciation

"Renunciation involves giving up competing relationships outside the communal group and individualistic, exclusive attachments within."[14] Close relationships like marriage, even between group members, can be viewed as a source of competition for an individual's commitment to the group as a whole, and so some communes and cults call for renunciation of such relationships. This is not the case with the early church and, thus, not with the author of Hebrews, who upholds marriage as an honorable and inviolable institution (13:4). He does, however, support some degree of renunciation of relationships with outsiders.

The author's use of the language of purity and holiness encourages separation (both ideological and social) from non-Christians. The members of the group are "those who are sanctified" (2:11; see also 10:10, 14) and "holy ones" (3:1; 6:10; 13:24), people set apart from the mass of humanity for special access to God.[15] They are also identified as "the people of God" (4:9), those who were "called" (9:15), a group thus set apart from competing political bodies by divine decree. The author's reminders of the sect's social history also encourage

14. Kanter, *Commitment*, 73.

15. The believers' access to God is itself a great privilege and a sign of their honor, even if this presently goes unrecognized. The author confers the exceptional dignity of the Jewish high priest on the believing community, since they now enjoy full access to the throne of grace (4:16; cf. 10:19–20). Indeed, the quality of this access exceeds that to which even the priests are entitled (13:10). Implicit in this is a claim for the greater honor of the believers on the basis of this greater privilege.

continued separation from outsiders. The author opens the old wounds of the believers' past experience of persecution, shaming, and dispossession at the hands of their hostile neighbors, undermining any aspirations of peaceful coexistence with a society that has rejected them and, perhaps more importantly, does not share their hope for the "better and lasting" possessions of God's realm (10:34). What partnership can there be between the Christians and the unbelieving society? The author's reminders of past persecution serve not only, then, to recall the believers' investment, but also to facilitate their ongoing renunciation of the larger society that also renounced them.[16]

The author's interest in establishing Jesus' superiority to the mediator figures (and the entire cultic system) of non-Christian Judaism may serve the goals of fostering renunciation, and thus commitment to the sect, as well. While apostasy to Judaism is probably not the overriding problem, the author may nevertheless use this line of argumentation to reawaken the community's sectarian consciousness over against the parent body, namely the non-Christian Jewish ethnos. The intellectual contrast between the old covenant (with its apparatus and personnel) and the new has a social dimension that comes to clearest expression in the us-versus-them contrast of 13:10: "We have an altar from which those who minister in the tabernacle have no authority to eat." Bryan Wilson observed that "the schismatic sect tends to be vigorous as long as its protest against the parent body remains significant."[17] The expository sections of Hebrews 1–10—the

16. Compare Elliott, *Social-Scientific Criticism*, 113–14; Neitz, *Charisma*, 160.

17. Wilson, "Analysis," 7.

most thoroughgoing specimen of apologetics in the New Testament—would certainly reinvigorate the sect's awareness of why it exists as an entity separate from the plausibility structures of non-Christian Judaism, as well as fuel the community's renunciation of the past religious history (whether or not it was ethnically their own) in order to strengthen their commitment to the present form of God's revelation in Jesus and its plausibility structures.

One of the macro-images that the author uses to depict the life of "faith" is the image of pilgrimage, even more specifically, a ritual pilgrimage—a "rite of passage" at a cosmic level. As the path of this pilgrimage takes one out from the comfortable places of society into and beyond the margins of the same, it is an image that also nurtures ongoing renunciation as it continues to reinforce the detachment of the community members from aspirations toward being "at home" in society, thus strengthening their commitment to the group. "Faith" itself entails refusing to call this world (meaning, the social structures beyond the sect) one's home. Faith entails a renunciation of native privileges and an exodus, a "going out" and a refusal to turn back, just as it did for Abraham (11:8–10, 13–16) and Moses (11:24–27). It means accepting marginalization in regard to the social structures of the present order of the dominant culture (as it did for the heroes of faith described in 11:35–38), knowing that this marginalization means going out to the place where, in communion with one another (see below), they will encounter their Lord who leads them on to their heavenly homeland:

> Therefore Jesus, in order to make the people sacred
> by means of his own blood, suffered outside the city
> gate. Let us, then, go out to him outside the camp,

bearing the reproach that fell on him, because here
we have no lasting city, but we are looking for the
one that is about to come. (13:12–14)

Communion

The positive counterpart to renunciation is communion,
"bringing members into meaningful contact with the collective whole, so that they experience the fact of oneness with
the group and develop a 'we-feeling.'"[18] The experience of past
persecution from outsiders and ongoing tension and conflict
as the author recalls it (10:32–34; 13:13) not only emphasizes
the boundaries between the Christian group and other social
bodies; it also binds the insiders together more closely as they
rely so much more on one another for affective and material
support, and identify so much the more with one another.[19]
The group experienced this "oneness" and "we-feeling" most
certainly during that time of persecution and thereafter, as
they cared for and were cared for by other group members as
if by family (6:9–10; 10:32–34).

The author continues to nurture the experience of communion by speaking of them in terms of a kinship group.
They are "God's household" (3:6) and God's "many sons
and daughters" (2:10, 14; 12:5–10), "brothers and sisters" to
Christ and to one another (2:11; 3:1, 12; 10:19; 13:22). They
are joined by a common genealogy (as God's "children," 2:10,
and "Abraham's descendants," 2:16) into a single family—a
family, moreover, enjoying a share in the honor of its divine
Head of the household. Their common bond is spoken of also

18. Kanter, *Commitment*, 73.

19. Ibid., 102; Elliott, *Social-Scientific Criticism*, 144.

in non-kinship terms, as "holy partners in a heavenly calling" (3:1) and as "Christ's partners" (3:14). As members renounce every aspect of "at-homeness" in the larger society, they continue to find that home with one another. Thus what John Elliott observed in connection with 1 Peter is also true of the Letter to the Hebrews:

> This ideology of the Christian community as the household of God served as a means for promoting internal sectarian cohesion and commitment while at the same time distinguishing and insulating the Christian in-group from other social groups, including Jews, other cults, and voluntary associations, as well as from the pretensions of imperial propaganda celebrating the emperor as "father of the fatherland" (*pater patriae*).[20]

Since they are God's family, the author exhorts them to behave as family, to take on the roles and responsibilities of family one for the other. By showing "brotherly and sisterly love" for one another (13:1), opening their homes to Christians from outside the local chapter (13:2; cf. 11:31), reaching out to their fellow members in dire need (13:3), and rendering one another mutual service (13:16; 6:10), they will enhance their sense of solidarity—the "we-feeling" that Kanter placed at the core of community.[21] The author affirms the "regularized group contact"[22] of the worship services (10:25), which are also the occasions for contact with the sacred ("approaching the throne of grace," 4:16; cf. 10:22), and calls for more personal and vital

20. Elliott, *Social-Scientific Criticism*, 85; see Elliott, *Home for the Homeless*, 174–80.

21. Compare Elliott, *Home for the Homeless*, 149, in regard to 1 Peter.

22. Kanter, *Commitment*, 98.

interaction between members of the group, as we have seen (3:12–13; 10:24; 12:15–16), all of which further nurtures the process of engendering commitment through communion.

Mortification and Transcendence

Very closely related to renunciation is the mechanism of mortification, which "involves . . . the exchanging of a former identity for one defined and formulated by the group."[23] As the label itself suggests, this process has to do with a group member's "dying" in some respect to the person he or she was prior to entering the group (and perhaps continuing to do so after becoming a member of the group), "reassessing one's previous life, to undo those parts of oneself one wishes to change."[24] Mortification is a process that one finds heavily and explicitly used in certain Pauline texts (e.g., Rom 6:1–14; Gal 2:19–20; 5:24; Col 3:5–17). It is part of the symbolism of the ritual of baptism discussed above in chapter 2 and recalled twice by the author of Hebrews (6:2; 10:22). It is reflected also in the reminder of the "repentance from dead works" that formed part of the foundation of the community members' conversion and resocialization, with the early Christian preachers helping the audience to identify what those "dead works" were from which the audience must dissociate themselves.[25] Nevertheless, mortification appears to be at most an ancillary strategy in the author's discourse.

Transcendence, on the other hand, plays a more prominent role in Hebrews. Transcendence "is a process whereby an

23. Ibid., 74.

24. Ibid., 73 (modified for inclusive language).

25. This appears again in the author's discussion of the effectiveness of Jesus' death to "cleanse our conscience from dead works" (9:14).

individual . . . surrender[s] to the higher meaning contained in the group and submit[s] to something beyond himself" or herself.[26] The author twice reminds the hearers of their own personal experience of this "something beyond" in the form of their encounter with God's Holy Spirit and its manifestations (2:4; 6:4–5). The audience would probably not deny the subjective and intersubjective reality of these experiences, which provide an experiential basis for the legitimacy of the new view of the cosmos and its destiny that they embraced in connection therewith.

We return at this point to the author's macro-image of the ritual journey for which the group members have been fitted (being cleansed in body and conscience by the waters of baptism and the blood of Jesus), and which is now "in progress" for them. Jesus pioneered this journey by going "outside the city gates" to suffer execution as a lawbreaker, bearing abuse, disgrace, and hostility (Heb 13:12). In the sight of God, however, this death completed a ritual act, just as the bodies of sacrificial animals were carried "outside the camp" for burning, completing the relevant ritual (Heb 13:11; Lev 4:12; 6:11; 16:27). The believers' journey began for them by following Christ, their forerunner, "outside the camp," when they sacrificed their place of belonging in human society and accepted being pushed into the margins because of their deviant confession (10:32–34, etc.). The place "outside the camp," however, is also the place where God is encountered and, thus, the transcendent experienced. Because of the sinfulness of the people, God ordered the tent of meeting to be moved "outside the camp" (Exod 33:1–7). As it was with the type, so it holds true with the antitype.

26. Kanter, *Commitment*, 74.

As the audience leaves the places of "at-homeness" in the world, following Jesus, they have moved into a sacral space where God's presence is found. Their movement out from the "camp" of the larger society at the same time means "approaching the throne of grace with boldness" (4:14–16) and drawing near to the threshold of the "heavenly sanctuary" that they may soon enter "with boldness by the blood of Jesus" (10:19). Even though their move "outside the camp" means "bearing Christ's reproach" here and now, it is at the same time a sacred journey into the places where God is to be met here and now en route to the heavenly Holy Place where God's presence will be enjoyed in full forever, still following Jesus, their forerunner (6:19–20).

Thus the author makes the common, even the degrading and marginalizing, holy. The experience of marginalization and social shaming is transcended, becoming a ritual journey out from the camp (where sin excludes the presence of a holy God) into the sacred spaces where God is encountered. The place "outside the camp" is the place inside the house where the congregation gathers. As group members travel through their city to meet together once again in a gathering that earns them their neighbors' rejection and censure, they are traveling toward the foot of "Mount Zion, the city of the living God, Heavenly Jerusalem." As they begin their liturgy together, they are joined in that sacred space by "innumerable angels singing a festival hymn," by "the assembly of the firstborn whose names are registered in the heavens," by "God, the judge of all, and . . . the spirits of the righteous who have been perfected," and by Jesus himself (12:22–24). As they continue in the same direction, persevering in their association with one another and with the name of Jesus, and thus moving forward in the direction that leads to the continued experience of shame and marginalization within the host society, they are moving toward their heavenly homeland, the city in which they will be enfranchised eternally (11:11–16; 13:14).

Beyond the transcendent experience of joining in the worship of the heavenly sanctuary and the assembly of the "communion of saints" in the gathering of the local house church or churches, the audience is invited to experience transcendence in two other respects as well. First, the author invites them to transcend the present moment by seeing their own journey in the greater context of the parade of the heroes of faith, the "people of God" in every generation (11:1–40). Second, and perhaps most prominently (indeed, from the very opening of the sermon), the author fixes the audience's mental eyes on the glorified Jesus, in whom the human condition itself is transcended. Jesus exists now in glory beyond death, living an "indestructible life" (2:6–9; 7:16); those who follow their pioneer will share in such a life as well, sharing also in the glory that radiates from the Son, the firstborn of many "sons and daughters" that he leads on to glory beyond death (2:10). As the audience fixes its eyes on Jesus (12:2) and identifies with him, they are empowered to overcome the present limitations of a life subject to suffering by focusing on the one who has been exalted above all (2:5–9).

Conclusion: Hebrews and the Problem of "Social Engineering"

Peter Berger speaks of the challenge of "social engineering" facing the person who "wishes to maintain the reality of a particular religious system."[27] It is not enough to have a plausible model of the cosmos, how it works, and where it is going (if anywhere); one must also have a social body that will keep creating and re-creating this image of the world for one another (i.e., a plausibility structure). The author of Hebrews writes within an environment of competing world-views and plausibility structures, with the latter interacting in some powerful, persuasive, even coercive ways. The audience, indeed, used to belong to the plausibility structure that sup-ported a rather different view of the cosmos (and, thus, a dif-ferent view of what kinds of lived practices were appropriate in such a cosmos). Some formerly participated in the plausibility structure that upheld the belief in the traditional gods of the city (perhaps including both the Greco-Roman pantheon and local, indigenous gods) and in the ideology of Roman rule, and thus engaged in those practices that upheld the interests of city and empire. Some formerly participated in the plau-sibility structure of the local Jewish community, engaging in those practices that upheld the Jewish people's interest in the covenant that defined them as a distinctive people.

Their conversion to the Christian group led to their withdrawal from these plausibility structures, involving them in disengagement from the practices that continued to sup-port their neighbors' own worldview and engagement in new practices that challenged these outright. This led, in turn, to some "social engineering" on the part of those neighbors. This took the form of applying social pressure to the deviant members of their plausibility structures (i.e., the Christians) with a view to "correcting" the deviants and drawing them

27. Berger, *Sacred Canopy*, 48.

back into the plausibility structure, at the same time reaffirm-
ing their own commitment to their worldview and ethos by
acting forcefully to reject the new attachments and practices
embraced by the deviants, and staving off further defections
to the Christian group by making an example of those who
had defected already.

The converts boldly persevered in their new commitment to the new social body, the *ekklēsia* of God, in the face
of this social pressure, but the steady pressure and experience
of living in the margins have begun to erode commitment
to the point that some have pulled back from the plausibility structure of the Christian gospel, presumably to return to
participate in the plausibility structures of either the dominant Greco-Roman population (or other indigenous Gentile
population) or the Jewish subculture. Now the author of
Hebrews crafts a sermon to effect some social engineering of
his own. His principal aim is to strengthen commitment to the
Christian group among those who are wavering, who might
themselves be moving toward defection (thus eroding the
Christian plausibility structure further, and jeopardizing ex-
ponentially the commitment of those who remain thereafter).

He gives extensive attention to insulating them from the
force of the social pressure they have endured and still endure,
both by encouraging them to "despise shame" and by presenting interpretive frames on their experience (God's formative
discipline; a wrestling match or race against sin and a society
characterized by sin and hostility toward God) that motivate
persevering and disincentivize yielding to the pressure.

He further utilizes a fundamental social institution with
its roles and scripts—the institution of patronage and its core
value of reciprocity—to heighten the value of the hearers'

experience since joining the Christian group (i.e., as entering into a grace relationship with the God of the cosmos and being privileged with experiencing God's favors and receiving God's promises) and to prioritize fulfilling their obligations as grateful recipients of favor. This, too, incentivizes persevering in commitment to and association with the Christian group as both a noble and advantageous response to Deity, while disincentivizing yielding to social pressure from outside as a course of action that shows contempt for God's patronage and gifts—testifying that neither is worth the price of loyalty and witness to God's generosity.

Finally, the author gives specific attention to the boundaries that mark the "court of opinion" whose verdicts of honorable and disgraceful ultimately matter. He vests the group's opinion with the authority of the divine, insofar as the former grounds its judgments in the sacred tradition of the Jewish Scriptures, the teaching of Jesus, and the apostolic proclamation. The "family of God" is the primary kinship group; those "sanctified" to enter God's eternal presence are *de facto* set apart from the unsanctified outsiders, who remain hostile to God and the supreme broker of that God's favor, Jesus. The author of Hebrews is also seen to have incorporated most of the commitment mechanisms identified in Kanter's model, particularly relying on the elements of investment, renunciation, communion, and transcendence to stimulate heightened commitment to the Christian sect among its members.

By means of this multifaceted strategy, the author seeks to help his audience accept their new social location—members of a sectarian movement in the margins of both the majority Greco-Roman culture and the Jewish ethnic subculture—as a place to which they have moved in response to God's call and Jesus' sanctifying action, and as a place from which they will enter the heavenly realm to be enfranchised in their own city and lasting homeland, the Heavenly Jerusalem. Though for the remainder of life in this transient world it means the experience of "bearing reproach" for the sake of Christ, the audience can transcend that experience through the hope of sharing in Christ's glory when they arrive, at last, where he has gone "as a forerunner on their behalf" (6:19–20). By assuring the perseverance of the plausibility structure (the *ekklēsia*), the author also assures that the community's counter-witness to "the way the cosmos is"—their witness to the One God in a polytheistic world and to a kingdom where self-sacrifice and other-centered service leads to a place at "the top," at God's right hand—will continue to be supported and voiced boldly, providing an alternative to the witness of the dominant culture and its celebrations of the apotheosis of power and violence.

Bibliography

Adkins, Arthur W. *Merit and Responsibility: A Study in Greek Values.* Oxford: Clarendon, 1960.

Aitken, Ellen B. "Portraying the Temple in Stone and Text: The Arch of Titus and the Epistle to the Hebrews." In *Hebrews: Contemporary Methods—New Insights*, edited by Gabriela Gelardini, 131–48. Leiden: Brill, 2005.

Attridge, Harold W. *The Epistle to the Hebrews.* Philadelphia: Fortress, 1989.

Attridge, H. W. "Paraenesis in a Homily (λόγος παρακλήσεως): The Possible Location of, and Socialization in, the 'Epistle to the Hebrews.'" *Semeia* 50 (1990) 211–26.

Bainbridge, William, and Rodney Stark. "Sectarian Tension." *RRelRes* 22 (1980) 105–24.

Barclay, J. M. G. "Mirror-Reading a Polemical Epistle: Galatians as a Test Case." *JSNT* 31 (1987) 73–93.

Barrett, C. K. "The Eschatology of the Epistle to the Hebrews." In *The Background of the New Testament and Its Eschatology*, edited by W. D. Davies and D. Daube, 363–93. Cambridge: Cambridge University Press, 1954.

Bateman, Herbert W., IV. *Early Jewish Hermeneutics and Hebrews 1:5–13.* New York: P. Lang, 1997.

Berger, Peter L. *The Sacred Canopy.* New York: Doubleday, 1967.

Berger, Peter L., and T. Luckmann. *The Social Construction of Reality.* New York: Anchor, 1967.

Boissevain, Jeremy. *Friends of Friends: Networks, Manipulators and Coalitions.* New York: St. Martin's, 1974.

Bruce, F. F. *The Epistle to the Hebrews.* Rev. ed. NICNT. Grand Rapids: Eerdmans, 1990.

Buchanan, George W. *To The Hebrews.* AB 36. Garden City, NY: Doubleday, 1970.

Büchsel, F. "Hebräerbrief." In *Religion in Geschichte und Gegenwart. Band II*, edited by H. Gunkel and L Zscharnack, 1669–73. 2nd ed. Tübingen: Möhr, 1928.

Carlston, C. "The Vocabulary of Perfection in Philo and Hebrews." In *Unity and Diversity in New Testament Theology*, edited by R. A. Guelich. Grand Rapids: Eerdmans, 1978.

Cockerill, Gareth. *The Epistle to the Hebrews*. NICNT. Grand Rapids: Eerdmans, 2012.

Cosby, M. R. *The Rhetorical Composition and Function of Hebrews 11 in Light of Example Lists in Antiquity*. Macon, GA: Mercer University Press, 1988.

———. "The Rhetorical Composition of Hebrews 11." *JBL* 107 (1988) 257–73.

Craddock, F. B. "Hebrews." In *The New Interpreter's Bible*, edited by Leander Keck, 12:1–174. Nashville: Abingdon, 1998.

Croy, N. C. *Endurance in Suffering: Hebrews 12:1–13 in Its Rhetorical, Religious, and Philosophical Contexts*. SNTSMS. Cambridge: Cambridge University Press, 1998.

D'Angelo, M. R. *Moses in the Letter to the Hebrews*. Missoula, MT: Scholars, 1979.

Danker, Frederick W. *Benefactor: Epigraphic Study of a Graeco-Roman and New Testament Semantic Field*. St. Louis: Clayton, 1982.

Derrett, J. D. M. *Jesus's Audience*. New York: Seabury, 1977.

DeSilva, David A. *4 Maccabees: Introduction and Commentary on the Greek Text*. Lieden: Brill, 2006.

———. *Despising Shame: Honor Discourse and Community Maintenance in the Epistle to the Hebrews*. Atlanta: Scholars Press, 1995; 2nd rev. ed., Atlanta: Society of Biblical Literature, 2008.

———. "Exchanging Favor for Wrath: Apostasy in Hebrews and Patron-Client Relations." *JBL* 115 (1996) 91–116.

———. "Hebrews 6:4–8: A Socio-Rhetorical Investigation." *TynBul* 50 (1999) 33–57, 225–36.

———. *Honor, Patronage, Kinship & Purity: Unlocking New Testament Culture*. Downers Grove, IL: InterVarsity, 2000.

———. *The Hope of Glory: Honor Discourse and New Testament Interpretation*. Collegeville, MN: Liturgical, 1999.

———. *An Introduction to the New Testament: Contexts, Methods & Ministry Formation*. Downers Grove, IL: InterVarsity, 2004.

———. *Perseverance in Gratitude: A Socio-Rhetorical Commentary on the Epistle "to the Hebrews."* Grand Rapids: Eerdmans, 2000.

De Ste. Croix, G. E. M. "Suffragium: From Vote to Patronage." *British Journal of Sociology* 5 (1954) 33–48.

De Vos, Craig S. *Church and Community Conflicts: The Relationships of the Thessalonian, Corinthian and Philippian Churches with Their Wider Civic Communities.* Atlanta: Scholars, 1999.

Douglas, Mary. *Purity and Danger: An Analysis of Concepts of Pollution and Taboo.* London: Routledge and Kegan Paul, 1966.

Durkheim, Emile. *The Elementary Forms of the Religious Life.* Translated by J. W. Swain. New York: Free Press, 1965.

Eisenbaum, Pamela M. *The Jewish Heroes of Christian History: Hebrews 11 in Literary Context.* Atlanta: Scholars, 1997.

Eisenstadt, S. N., and Louis Roniger. *Patrons, Clients and Friends: Interpersonal Relations and the Structure of Trust in Society.* Cambridge: Cambridge University, 1984.

Eliade, Mircea. *Patterns in Comparative Religion.* New York: Sheed & Ward, 1958.

Ellingworth, Paul. *The Epistle to the Hebrews.* NIGTC. Grand Rapids: Eerdmans, 1993.

———. "Hebrews and 1 Clement: Literary Dependence or Common Tradition." *BZ* 23 (1979) 262–69.

Elliott, John H. *A Home for the Homeless: A Social-Scientific Criticism of 1 Peter, Its Situation and Strategy, with a New Introduction.* Minneapolis: Fortress, 1990.

———. "Patron-Client Relations and the New Community in Luke-Acts." In *The Social World of Luke-Acts*, edited by J. H. Neyrey, 241–68. Peabody, MA: Hendrickson, 1991.

———. "Patronage and Clientism in Early Christian Society." *Forum* 3 (1987) 39–48.

———. *What Is Social-Scientific Criticism?* Minneapolis: Fortress, 1990.

Filson, F. V. *"Yesterday": A Study of Hebrews in the Light of Chapter 13.* London: SCM, 1967.

Geertz, Clifford. *The Interpretation of Cultures: Selected Essays.* New York: Basic Books, 1973.

Gelardini, Gabriela, ed. *Hebrews. Contemporary Methods—New Insights.* Leiden: Brill, 2005.

Gleason, Randall C. "The Old Testament Background of the Warning in Hebrews 6:4–8." *BSac* 155 (1998) 62–91.

Guthrie, George H. *Hebrews.* NIVAC. Grand Rapids: Zondervan, 1998.

———. *The Structure of Hebrews: A Text-Linguistic Analysis.* Leiden: Brill, 1994.

Gyllenberg, R. "Die Composition des Hebräerbriefs." *Svensk Exegetisk Årsbok* 22–23 (1957–58) 137–47.

Hagner, Donald. A. *Hebrews*. Rev. ed. NIBCNT. Peabody, MA: Hendrickson, 1990.

———. *The Use of the Old and New Testaments in Clement of Rome.* Leiden: Brill, 1973.

Hamm, D. "Faith in the Epistle to the Hebrews: The Jesus Factor." *CBQ* 52 (1990) 270–91.

Harrington, Daniel J. "Second Testament Exegesis and the Social Sciences: A Bibliography." *BTB* 18 (1988) 77–85.

Hengel, Martin. *Crucifixion in the Ancient World.* Philadelphia: Fortress, 1977.

Héring, Jean. *The Epistle to the Hebrews.* Translated by A. W. Heathcote. London: Epworth, 1970.

Holmberg, Bengt. *Paul and Power: The Structure of Authority in the Primitive Church as Reflected in the Pauline Epistles.* Philadelphia: Fortress, 1978.

———. *Sociology and the New Testament: An Appraisal.* Minneapolis: Fortress, 1990.

Horrell, David G. *Social-Scientific Approaches to New Testament Interpretation.* Edinburgh: T. & T. Clark, 1999.

———. *The Social Ethos of the Corinthian Correspondence: Interests and Ideology from 1 Corinthians to 1 Clement.* Edinburgh: T. & T. Clark, 1996.

Hughes, Philip E. *A Commentary on the Epistle to the Hebrews.* Grand Rapids: Eerdmans, 1977.

Hurst, L. D. *The Epistle to the Hebrews: Its Background of Thought.* Cambridge: Cambridge University, 1990.

Jewett, Robert. *A Letter to Pilgrims: A Commentary on the Epistle to the Hebrews.* New York: Pilgrim, 1981.

Johnson, Luke T. *Hebrews: A Commentary.* NTL. Louisville: Westminster John Knox, 2006.

Johnson, Benton. "Church and Sect Revisited." *JSSR* 28 (1970) 124–37.

Kanter, R. M. *Commitment and Community: Communes and Utopias in Sociological Perspective.* Cambridge, MA: Harvard University Press, 1972.

Karrer, Martin. *Der Brief an die Hebräer: Kapitel 1,1—5,10.* Gütersloh: Gütersloher; Würzburg: Echter, 2002.

Käsemann, Ernst. *The Wandering People of God: An Investigation of the Letter to the Hebrews.* Minneapolis: Augsburg, 1984 [1961].

Kee, Howard C. *Knowing the Truth: A Sociological Approach to New Testament Interpretation*. Minneapolis: Fortress, 1989.

Kennedy, George A. *New Testament Interpretation through Rhetorical Criticism*. Chapel Hill: University of North Carolina Press, 1984.

———. *Progymnasmata: Greek Textbooks of Prose Composition and Rhetoric*. Writings from the Greco-Roman World 10. Atlanta: Society of Biblical Literature, 2003.

Koester, Craig. *The Epistle to the Hebrews*. AB 36. Garden City, NY: Doubleday, 2001.

Lane, William L. *Hebrews 1–8*. WBC 47A. Dallas: Word, 1991.

———. *Hebrews 9–13*. WBC 47B. Dallas: Word, 1991.

Laub, F. "Verkündigung und Gemeindeamt: Die Autorität der ἡγούμενοι Hebr 13,7.17.24." *SNTSU* 6–7 (1981–82) 169–90.

Lehne, Susanne. *The New Covenant in Hebrews*. Sheffield: JSOT Press, 1990.

Levick, Barbara. *The Government of the Roman Empire: A Sourcebook*. London: Croom Helm, 1985.

Levine, Baruch A. *Leviticus*. JPS Torah Commentary. Philadelphia: Jewish Publication Society, 1989.

Lindars, Barnabas. "The Rhetorical Structure of Hebrews." *NTS* 35 (1989) 382–406.

———. *The Theology of the Letter to the Hebrews*. Cambridge: Cambridge University, 1991.

Long, Thomas. *Hebrews*. Interpretation. Louisville: Westminster John Knox, 1997.

Lünemann, Gerhard. *Kritisch exegetisches Handbuch über den Hebräerbrief*. KEK. Göttingen: Vandenhoeck & Ruprecht, 1878.

Mack, Burton L. *Rhetoric and the New Testament*. Minneapolis: Fortress, 1990.

MacMullen, Ramsay. *Paganism in the Roman Empire*. New Haven, CT: Yale University Press, 1981.

Malina, Bruce. *The New Testament World: Insights from Cultural Anthropology*. Louisville: Westminster John Knox, 1993 [1981].

Malina, Bruce, and J. H. Neyrey. "Honor and Shame in Luke-Acts: Pivotal Values of the Mediterranean World." In *The Social World of Luke-Acts: Models for Interpretation*, edited by J. H. Neyrey, 25–56. Peabody, MA: Hendrickson, 1991.

Marx, Karl, and Friedrich Engels, *On Religion*. Edited by Reinhold Niebuhr. Classics in Religious Studies 3. Atlanta: Scholars, 1964.

Meeks, Wayne A. *The First Urban Christians*. 2nd ed. New Haven, CT: Yale University Press, 2003.

Michel, Otto. *Der Brief an die Hebräer.* 12th ed. KEK. Göttingen: Vandenhoeck & Ruprecht, 1960.

Milgrom, Jacob. *Leviticus 1–16.* AB 3. New York: Doubleday, 1991.

Mitchell, Alan C. *Hebrews.* SP 13. Collegeville, MN: Liturgical, 2007.

Moffatt, James. *A Critical and Exegetical Commentary on the Epistle to the Hebrews.* ICC. Edinburgh: T. & T. Clark, 1924.

Montefiore, Hugh. *A Commentary on the Epistle to the Hebrews.* HNTC. New York: Harper, 1964.

Moxnes, Halvor, editor. *Constructing Early Christian Families: Family as Social Reality and Metaphor.* London: Routledge, 1997.

————. "Honor and Shame." *BTB* 23 (1993) 167–76.

————. "Honour and Righteousness in Romans." *JSNT* 32 (1988) 61–77.

Muir, Stephen. "The Anti-Imperial Rhetoric of Hebrews 1.3: χαρακτήρ as a 'Double-Edged Sword.'" In *A Cloud of Witnesses: The Theology of Hebrews in Its Ancient Contexts,* edited Richard Bauckham et al., 170–86. Edinburgh: T. & T. Clark, 2008.

Neitz, M. J. *Charisma and Community.* New Brunswick, NJ: Transaction Books, 1987.

Nelson, Richard D. *Raising Up a Faithful Priest: Community and Priesthood in a Biblical Theology.* Louisville: Westminster John Knox, 1993.

Neyrey, J. H. "The Idea of Purity in Mark's Gospel." *Semeia* 35 (1986) 91–128.

————. "Loss of Wealth, Loss of Family and Loss of Honor: A Cultural Interpretation of the Original Four Makarisms." In *Modelling Early Christianity: Social-Scientific Studies of the New Testament in Its Context,* edited by Philip F. Esler, 134–58. London: Routledge, 1995.

O'Brien, Peter T. *The Letter to the Hebrews.* Pillar New Testament Commentary. Grand Rapids: Eerdmans, 2010.

Osiek, Carolyn, and David L. Balch. *Families in the New Testament World: Households and House Churches.* Louisville: Westminster John Knox, 1997.

Peterson, David. *Hebrews and Perfection: An Examination of the Concept of Perfection in the "Epistle to the Hebrews."* Cambridge: Cambridge University Press, 1982.

Pfitzner, Victor C. *Hebrews.* ACNT. Nashville: Abingdon, 1997.

————. *Paul and the Agon Motif: Traditional Athletic Imagery in the Pauline Literature.* Leiden: Brill, 1967.

Pitt-Rivers, Julian. "Honour and Social Status." In *Honour and Shame: The Values of Mediterranean Society,* edited by J. G. Peristiany, 21–77. London: Weidenfeld and Nicolson, 1965.

Robbins, Vernon K. *Exploring the Texture of Texts*. Valley Forge, PA: Trinity, 1996.

———. *The Tapestry of Early Christian Discourse: Rhetoric, Society and Ideology*. London: Routledge, 1996.

Roberts, Keith A. *Religion in Sociological Perspective*. Chicago: Dorsey, 1984.

———. "Toward a Generic Concept of Counter-Culture." *Sociological Focus* 11 (1978) 111–26.

Salevao, Iutisone. *Legitimation in the Letter to the Hebrews: The Construction and Maintenance of a Symbolic Universe*. Sheffield: Sheffield Academic, 2002.

Saller, R. P. *Personal Patronage under the Early Empire*. Cambridge: Cambridge University Press, 1982.

Scholer, J. M. *Proleptic Priests: Priesthood in the Epistle to the Hebrews*. Sheffield: JSOT Press, 1991.

Spicq, Ceslaus. *L'Épître aux Hébreux*. 2 vols. Paris: Gabalda, 1953.

Stagg, Frank. "The Abused Aorist." *JBL* 91 (1972) 222–31.

Stark, Rodney, and William Bainbridge. "Of Churches, Sects, and Cults: Preliminary Concepts for a Theory of Religious Movements." *JSSR* 18 (1979) 117–33.

Theissen, Gerd. *The Social Setting of Pauline Christianity: Essays on Corinth*. Philadelphia: Fortress, 1982.

———. *Untersuchungen zum Hebräerbrief*. SNT 2. Gütersloh: Mohn, 1969.

Thompson, James W. *The Beginnings of Christian Philosophy: The Epistle to the Hebrews*. Washington, DC: Catholic Biblical Association of America, 1982.

———. *Hebrews*. Paideia. Grand Rapids: Baker Academic, 2008.

Trotter, A. H., Jr. *Interpreting the Epistle to the Hebrews*. Grand Rapids: Baker, 1997.

Turner, Victor. *The Ritual Process: Structure and Anti-Structure*. Ithaca, NY: Cornell University, 1969.

Verbrugge, Verlyn G. "Towards a New Interpretation of Hebrews 6:4–6." *CTJ* 15 (1980) 61–73.

Wallace-Hadrill, Andrew, editor. *Patronage in Ancient Society*. London: Routledge, 1989.

Wansink, Craig A. *Chained in Christ: The Experience and Rhetoric of Paul's Imprisonments*. Sheffield: Sheffield Academic, 1996.

Weber, Max. *Economy and Society: An Outline of Interpretive Sociology*. 3 vols. New York: Bedminster, 1968.

———. *The Sociology of Religion*. Boston: Beacon, 1963 [1922].

———. "The Three Types of Legitimate Rule." *Berkeley Publications in Society and Institutions* 4 (1958) 1–11.

Weiss, Hans-Friedrich. *Der Brief an die Hebräer*. 15th ed. KEK. Göttingen: Vandenhoeck & Ruprecht, 1991.

Westcott, B. F. *The Epistle to the Hebrews*. 3rd ed. London: Macmillan, 1920 [1903].

Williamson, Ronald. *Philo and the Epistle to the Hebrews*. Leiden: Brill, 1970.

———. "Platonism and Hebrews." *SJT* 16 (1963) 415–24.

Wilson, Bryan R. "An Analysis of Sect Development." In *Patterns of Sectarianism: Organization and Ideology in Social and Religious Movements*, edited by B. R. Wilson, 22–45. London: Heinemann, 1967.

Witherington, Ben, III. "The Influence of Galatians on Hebrews." *NTS* 37 (1991) 146–52.

———. *Letters and Homilies for Jewish Christians: A Socio-Rhetorical Commentary on Hebrews, James and Jude*. Downers Grove, IL: InterVarsity, 2007.

Worley, David R., Jr. "God's Faithfulness to Promise." PhD diss., Yale University, 1981.

Index of Ancient Texts

Index of Modern Authors

Index of Subjects